T0383520

THE GODS
& GODDESSES
OF GREECE
& ROME

A GUIDE TO THE CLASSICAL PANTHEON

The Gods & Goddesses of Greece & Rome

PHILIP MATYSZAK

CONTENTS

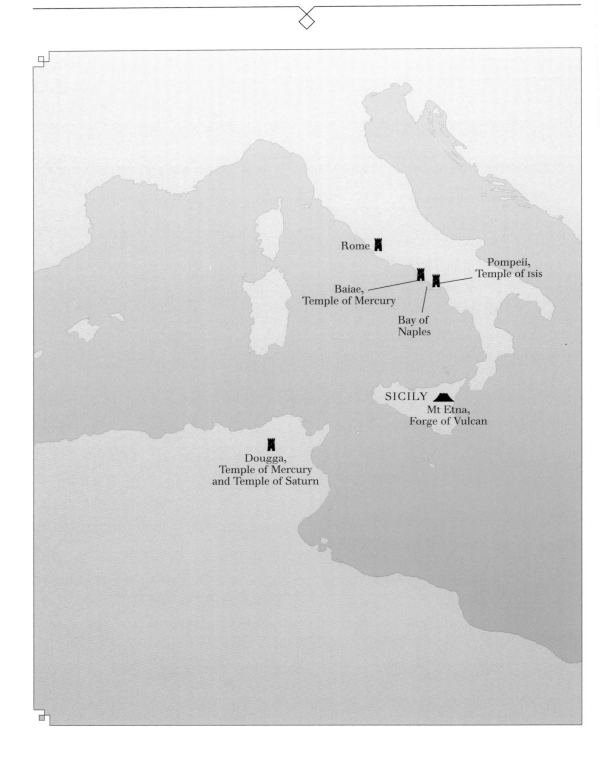

Rome

Pompeii,
Temple of Isis

Baiae,
Temple of Mercury

Bay of
Naples

SICILY

Mt Etna,
Forge of Vulcan

Dougga,
Temple of Mercury
and Temple of Saturn

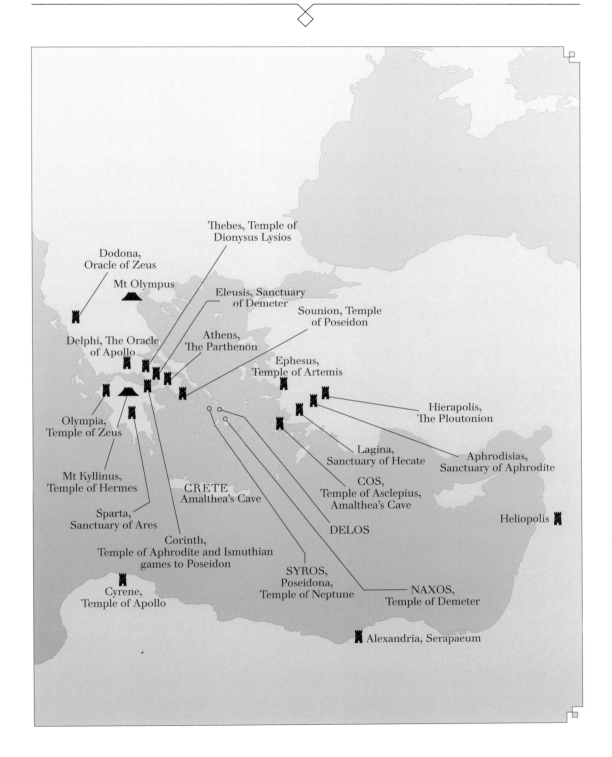

Dodona,
Oracle of Zeus

Mt Olympus

Thebes, Temple of
Dionysus Lysios

Eleusis, Sanctuary
of Demeter

Sounion, Temple
of Poseidon

Delphi, The Oracle
of Apollo

Athens,
The Parthenon

Ephesus,
Temple of Artemis

Hierapolis,
The Ploutonion

Olympia,
Temple of Zeus

Lagina,
Sanctuary of Hecate

Aphrodisias,
Sanctuary of Aphrodite

Mt Kyllinus,
Temple of Hermes

CRETE
Amalthea's Cave

COS,
Temple of Asclepius,
Amalthea's Cave

Heliopolis

Sparta,
Sanctuary of Ares

DELOS

Corinth,
Temple of Aphrodite and Ismuthian
games to Poseidon

SYROS,
Poseidona,
Temple of Neptune

NAXOS,
Temple of Demeter

Cyrene,
Temple of Apollo

Alexandria, Serapaeum

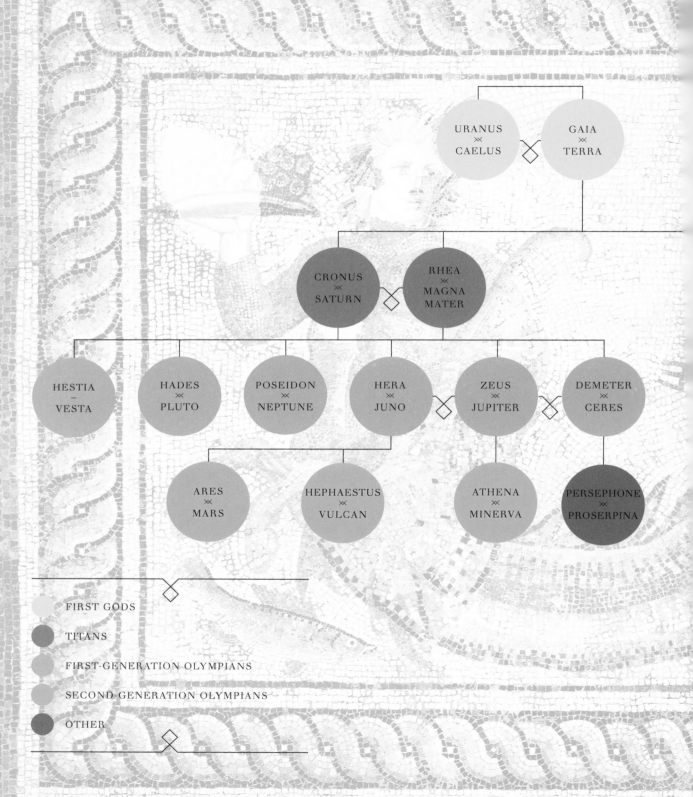

URANUS
×
CAELUS

GAIA
×
TERRA

CRONUS
×
SATURN

RHEA
×
MAGNA
MATER

HESTIA
–
VESTA

HADES
×
PLUTO

POSEIDON
×
NEPTUNE

HERA
×
JUNO

ZEUS
×
JUPITER

DEMETER
×
CERES

ARES
×
MARS

HEPHAESTUS
×
VULCAN

ATHENA
×
MINERVA

PERSEPHONE
×
PROSERPINA

FIRST GODS

TITANS

FIRST-GENERATION OLYMPIANS

SECOND-GENERATION OLYMPIANS

OTHER

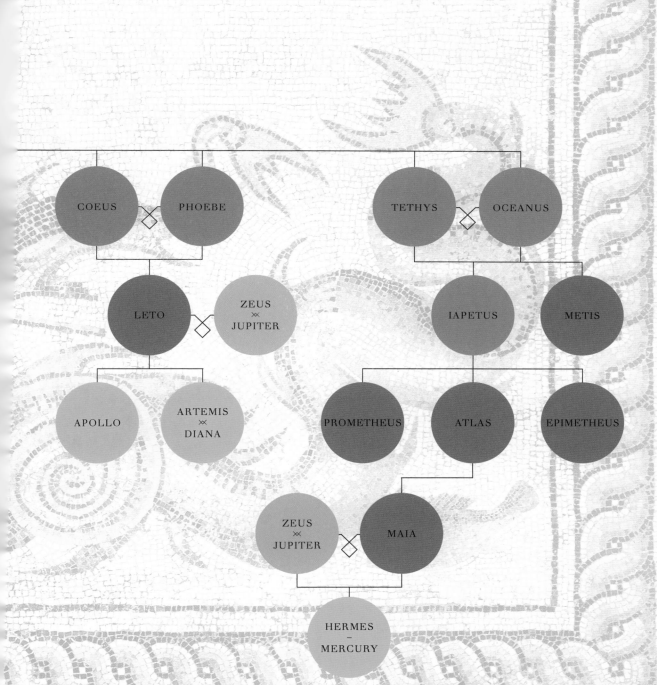

INTRODUCTION

Giulio Romano, detail of fresco from Sala dei Giganti (Chamber of Giants), Palazzo del Te, Mantua, 1532–34.

–

The Gigantomachy was a literally titanic struggle between the Olympian gods and the race of Giants who attempted to overthrow them. The battle came in the early days when the world was still emerging from chaos. This mood of brutal violence and confusion is captured in this fresco.

Understanding the Classical Gods

Ancient Greece and Rome have profoundly affected life, culture and thought in the modern world. Yet today in Europe, the former home of the Greek and Roman gods, beliefs about divinity are radically different from those in the ancient world. To understand the Greek and Roman gods, we must first forget almost everything we believe about the nature of the divine and start again.

Today the Vatican in Rome preaches one of the Abrahamic faiths, Christianity, in which God is a completely different order of being from humans: eternal and changeless, omnipotent and omnipresent. God is the 'creator of heaven and earth'. He (the Abrahamic god is male) resides in heaven, somewhere beyond the sky, and is a god of love. He is opposed by the Devil who, in his subterranean hell, is the incarnation of evil and the promoter of sin and moral turpitude. The words of God are written in holy books interpreted by clerics who may insist that disagreement with their tenets is heresy or blasphemy. Indeed, the Council of Nicaea in AD 325 was convened expressly for the purpose of standardizing the Christian faith and separating 'God's word' from heresy.

We consider Christianity here because it was one of the faiths that supplanted 'pagan' worship in most of the area once ruled by Rome. However, followers of other religions can also usefully compare their own understanding of divinity with the characteristics of the ancient gods that are described below. When seen from the perspective of modern theology, the gods and goddesses of Greece and Rome can seem silly, arbitrary and spitefully cruel and the myths that surround them merely a set of somewhat nonsensical stories.

Yet some seriously intelligent people in the ancient world believed in and devoutly worshiped these gods, not because they were irrational but because they viewed their gods from a completely different perspective – a perspective that must be approached without modern preconceptions.

For a start, the ancient gods were far from eternal and changeless – almost as much as the rest of us they were creatures of space and time. There are fairly detailed accounts of the birth of each god and comprehensive genealogies of their parents and descendants, and occasionally tales of their childhood and upbringing. The only reason we do not have accounts of their deaths is that ancient theology agrees with the modern that neither god nor man can truly die. However, fate ruled the lives of the gods just as it rules the lives of humans, and the ancients expected that when eventually the cosmos aged and died the gods would go down with it.

The ancient gods were also far from omnipotent – in fact, rather than being all-powerful, Zeus, the king of the gods, was as nervous as any other ancient autocrat about being supplanted by revolution or a usurper. The fact that Zeus came to power by overthrowing his predecessor after a brief but nasty war might

left

After Friedrich Thiersch, interior view of the Parthenon with statue of Athena Parthenos by Phidias, 1879.

—

This woodcut imagines the interior of the Parthenon on the Acropolis of Athens some time in the mid-fifth century BC. Dominating the space is a colossal (11.5m) statue of Athena, the maiden goddess (thea parthenos). In her hand Athena holds Nike, goddess of victory. The statue was winged as a wry acknowledgment that victory could take flight at any moment.

opposite

Antoine-Chrysostome Quatremère de Quincy, *Le Jupiter Olympien vu dans son trône*, 1814.

—

The master-work of the great Phidias was the 12m-tall statue of Zeus at Olympia, recognized as one of the Seven Wonders of the Ancient World. The statue was made of gold and ivory, and there was a pool of olive oil in front of it to keep the ivory from cracking and warping.

LE JUPITER OLYMPIEN,
VU DANS SON TRÔNE ET DANS L'INTERIEUR DE SON TEMPLE,

have had something to do with this. (Note that here we talk of the Greek Zeus rather than his Roman counterpart, Jupiter. Though conflated, in some ways Jupiter and Zeus were very different, as will be seen later.)

Nor were the gods all-seeing (hundred-eyed Argus Panoptes came close, but he was merely a supernatural being rather than a fully fledged god) and certainly they were not omnipresent – there are a multitude of cases where both mortals and gods got up to hijinks when another god was absent or sleeping. There were many occasions on which the polyamorous Zeus/Jupiter sneaked away from his wife to impregnate mortal lovers, and the infant Hermes/Mercury managed to steal an entire flock of cattle while their owner, Apollo, was not looking.

The gods did not create heaven and earth – in fact the ancient theory that the cosmos came spontaneously into being from primordial chaos is remarkably consistent with modern scientific thinking. Rather the classical gods are a creation of the earth – quite literally, as the earth is the physical manifestation of the goddess Gaia, the mother of all.

And on the topic of goddesses, let us note that the deities of Greece and Rome were male and female and, far from being asexual, they generally had remarkably diverse sex lives, which they enthusiastically enjoyed – the virgin goddesses Artemis, Athena and Hecate excepted. These sexual escapades lead us to another important point: while the Abrahamic God frowns upon moral turpitude, the ancient gods were in no position to do the same. Their lives were packed with vindictiveness, mendacity, adultery and dirty tricks by the dozen. Enforcing strict moral behaviour was not a part of the average god's portfolio. The gods did not require morality as a condition of their worship and indeed it would have been somewhat hypocritical had they done so.

The misdeeds of the gods have been documented in a massive corpus of ancient texts, which differ from holy books in significant ways. Principally these books are not the divinely revealed word of God – indeed one suspects that Zeus/Jupiter would prefer that they were not published at all – and they are not dogmatic. ('Dogma' is defined as those words of holy writ that are disputed only at the risk of one's immortal soul.)

Instead, the ancient texts describing the gods were written partly as a form of entertainment and anyone who felt that they could do better was welcome to try. This has considerably frustrated modern students of myth, as some gods are assigned

Terracotta antefix with Venus and Mars, Roman, late 1st century BC–early 1st century AD.

–

The Romans revered Mars as the father of Romulus and Remus and Venus as the ancestor of the Julian line. In mythology Mars and Venus were lovers and the parents of Fear and Terror (Phobos and Deimos, now moons of Mars).

different parents by different traditions, and beliefs about divinity evolved along with Greek and Roman society. (And not always for the better – females, divine and otherwise, tend to be much stronger characters in the older myths.) The classical playwright Euripides, for example, took considerable liberties with myths traditional in his day, and the result is what can best be described as a bifurcated canon, for Euripides was a good enough storyteller for his version to have partly replaced the older versions.

In short, the Greek myths that described the classical gods were open to reinterpretation and even extensive rewriting

as a changing world demanded different attributes of its deities. Gods occasionally adopted new roles as the demands of society shifted (for example, Neptune originally was a god of fountains and rivers until his conflation with Poseidon made him lord of the Roman sea). Indeed, ancient gods were subject to a form of theological Darwinism, in which older gods who could not adapt fell out of favour and other gods more suited to the times grew in popularity and were worshiped in their place. This flexibility contrasts strongly with the unchanging God of monotheistic faiths, the ostensibly unalterable content of their holy books and the fates of those who attempted to reinterpret – let alone rewrite – the Bible in medieval and early modern Europe.

This brings us to the elusive concept of a 'sin' as opposed to a 'crime'. Even in the modern world the two types of misdeed are not synonymous, for if merely the seven deadly sins of gluttony, lust, greed, wrath, sloth, envy and pride were arrestable offences the whole of humanity would be behind bars. Yet the

August Theodor Kaselowsky, *Tantalus and Sisyphus in Hades*, c. 1850.

–

Sisyphus (in the background) and Tantalus were both kings who offended the gods. Tantalus has given us the verb 'to tantalize' from his punishment of having food and drink close by but unavailable, and Sisyphus has given us a 'Sisyphean labour' for any task that is laborious and pointless. (Sisyphus had to push a boulder up a hill, but the boulder always rolled to the bottom before he finished.) It is disputable that the pair were actually punished in Hades, as myth places them in Tartarus, a deeper and darker place than the kingdom of Hades.

ancient world went further in being entirely innocent of the concept of sin. There were crimes certainly – committed by both gods and humans – but it was seldom possible to break the commandments of the gods without also breaking the laws of man.

Blasphemy was generally not in itself a crime since the ancients saw little point in punishing a blasphemer when the gods were capable of doing it themselves and doing it much better. However, because the gods were also somewhat indiscriminate in their choice of punishment and extremely careless of collateral damage, those living within the potential blast radius tended to urge blasphemers to move far, far away. In fact, almost all cases of religious persecution in antiquity were not from outrage at the religious beliefs of the persecuted but from fear of how the classical gods would react to insult – and some groups, especially the early Christians, were extremely rude.

Finally, the ancient equivalent of hell was the underworld, the kingdom of Hades, ruled by Pluto, the Lord of Many. His domain was not a place of punishment but the true home of mankind, where souls recently dead or those awaiting rebirth reflected, in a place of passionless quiet, upon their lives on earth and what they might do better next time. The destination for wrong-doers was Tartarus, a place in which only the most egregious offenders were sentenced to punishments which have become proverbial – the two best examples being Tantalus and Sisyphus.

So, having decided what the gods of Greece and Rome were not, we must now address the question of what they were – a question that has no single answer, because different individuals in the classical world held vastly different opinions and there was no sole authority to put them right. An ancient priest was more of a religious technician who made sure that the right animals were sacrificed to the correct god in the course of properly conducting the right rituals at the right time. Ancient priests preached no sermons and made no judgments about morality – how could they, since many ancient priests were also politicians?

The opinions of the average 'pagan' are very difficult to reconstruct, for most of what has survived are the views of a small, well-educated elite. Yet by and large that elite were scrupulously religious, and the little we do know about the wider population leads us to believe that the ordinary run of people were even more so.

overleaf
Giulio Romano and workshop, fresco with Orpheus in the Underworld, Palazzo del Te, Mantua, 1526–35.
–
The master musician Orpheus attempts to charm Hades and his wife Persephone into releasing his beloved Eurydice from the underworld. Despite the distressed condition of the painting, this is not ancient but from the workshop of Giulio Romano.

It is useful to think of the ancient gods not as superhuman beings but as the fundamental forces of the universe, and in this respect the fate of a Theban princess called Semele is instructive. She was the lover of Zeus, and Zeus had on this occasion assumed a human guise (his other disguises included a bull and a shower of gold). However, Semele knew that Zeus was far more than he currently appeared. In a spirit of scientific curiosity she tricked him into revealing his true nature – and was incinerated on the spot by the sheer power of the being who stood before her. For the classical gods did not merely represent the different forces of the universe – they were those forces, for all that they sometimes wore a human face.

Thus, for example, in his role as the god of order, Zeus/ Jupiter is the actual force of order – the reason why maths and physics work and why people wake up today in the same shape they went to bed in yesterday, and, indeed, why today follows yesterday in the first place. As the force of order, it is natural that this particular entity is the ruler of the other gods. (Zeus also picked up a multitude of other roles, while retaining his most ancient role as a weather god.)

Pothos Painter, bell krater with scene of sacrifice, Greek, c. 420 BC.

–

Bell kraters such as this elaborate urn were used for mixing wine with water at Greek dinner parties – Greeks seldom drank their wine undiluted. The vases often featured scenes with a religious or mythological theme, such as this scene of a goat sacrifice by the Athenian 'Pothos' painter. The painter's actual name is unknown, but several vases with his scenes of sacrifice have been found, including one with a picture of a beautiful participant whom the painter had labelled *pothos* – yearning.

Introduction

Demeter/Ceres is the force that turns a seed into grain – today she could be called 'hypogeal germination' without greatly affecting her role – and huge amounts of nitrates and other fertilizers are regularly sacrificed to her. Apollo is the power that allows us to appreciate beauty, art and music, while Athena/Minerva is the power of the rational intellect over panic and superstition. All the way through the ancient pantheon the gods embodied the forces that make the universe tick and the human aspect of these gods provided mortals with a means to interact with and influence those forces.

In short, people worshiped the classical gods because they most certainly existed, and still do today. The only question is whether these forces are self-aware, interested in human affairs and capable of actively intervening in them as the Greeks and Romans believed – but then agnostics and atheists have similar doubts about all gods everywhere. The classical gods have at least the advantage of being real – one can hardly doubt the existence of Boreas, the north wind, when he is blowing sleet down your neck. You can only ask whether he is blowing the sleet as a natural force or with intentional malice.

This view of the gods explains why they are depicted in myth as arbitrary and capricious – because that's how the forces of nature really are. It also explains why these forces are anthropomorphized with human traits – if you can persuade Jupiter not to strike you with a thunderbolt, or Aphrodite to grant you access to the lover of your dreams, then that is ever so much better than leaving matters to an impersonal, uncaring universe. Moreover, if the gods are to be persuadable, then they must be sufficiently human to be open to human suasion – after all, very few humans ask their god for justice rather than mercy. So the ancient gods were vulnerable to flattery, subject to trickery and disposed to sentimentality because their human worshipers preferred them that way.

Which leads to a final observation about the nature of worship, which was again very different from how we conceive of it today. The Romans, in their usual methodical fashion, summarized things best with what they called the *pax deorum*: the peace of the gods. This is not the peace (of mind) that the priest wishes upon his flock as they depart from worship, but the kind of peace one finds in international treaties. The classical gods protected their worshipers in exchange for the performance of civic rituals performed in their honour. As long as the gods got their due, they gave protection in return.

A worshiper was no more compelled or expected to 'believe' in his gods than citizens are required to believe in their mayor before they pay city taxes. And as for 'loving your God with all your heart and all your soul', well, a classical god would be as uncomfortable with such declarations of undying devotion as a mayor would be if a constituent expressed similar sentiments on a tax return.

The Greek and Roman gods and goddesses expected the peoples and cities under their protection to pay their dues. After that people could believe in and worship whomever and however they pleased, for the gods were mainly interested in their relationships with whole communities rather than individuals. This is one reason why almost everyone in myth is a god, royalty or an aristocrat – common folk rarely merited individual attention from the gods, and when they did get it, things usually ended badly for them.

This aspect of ancient gods, namely that they were patrons and protectors of the communities that worshiped them, partly explains the dearth of religious wars in antiquity. If a god worked well for a community, then its people saw no reason to persuade their neighbours – who were usually their enemies – to obtain the same benefits. In fact, the more misguided neighbouring communities were in their worship, the better.

Rather than proselytize, the Romans adopted the opposite approach. If the god of an enemy appeared particularly effective, they had a rite called *evocatio* by which Roman priests offered the enemy's deity a larger, better temple in Rome, convenient in its shops and amenities, and with more numerous and more enthusiastic worshipers. Throughout their history the gods of Rome had to share religious space with a host of imported gods.

And so, before we encounter the gods and goddesses of Greece and Rome, let us forget the silly caricatures depicted in modern films and books. It is only when we step back and see the gods from the viewpoint of the ancients that we realize we are dealing with a theology as sophisticated, coherent and worthy of respect as any other belief system.

The First Gods

If a god is not considered to be an eternal presence, then this raises the obvious question of that god's origin. The ancient Greeks gave considerable thought to this matter and later passed their conclusions on to the Romans, who adopted them

Fragment of bas-relief with Minerva and possibly Apollo, Roman, 100 BC–AD 100.
–
Minerva is immediately recognizable by her aegis breastplate and spear (and distinguishable from her Greek counterpart Athena by her Roman hairstyle and Roman legionary helmet with distinctive plume). A very similar depiction has been unearthed from Herculaneum.

wholesale. The consequence of this is that we have no uniquely Roman origin stories for the great gods.

By the time their beliefs enter the historical record, the Romans had gods of various kinds: some embodied natural forces, as did the Greek gods with whom their Roman counterparts rapidly merged; other Roman gods were the perfect form of a thing or activity. This second type has led to considerable mirth among monotheists who cannot understand why there should be, for example, a god of manure-spreading or a goddess of door hinges. However, the Roman approach makes more sense when we consider that Sterquilinus is the personification of manure-spreading done exactly right. And mock the goddess of door hinges at your peril, for Cardea's portfolio includes the little valves that control the flow of blood within our hearts, and cardiac arrest is no joke.

So Sterquilinus came into being as soon as the first person realized it was a good idea to spread manure upon farmland, and to spread it well, and Cardea came into being at the same time as the first hinge. Yet the origin of these lesser gods does not work for the great gods who make up the earth, the sea and the sky. These gods needed more comprehensive explanations, and to these stories the Greeks applied a wonderful mix of fantasy and rigorous logic.

Let us start as did the universe, with a state of complete chaos. Modern science calls this the Singularity and the Greeks called it the World Egg. Both modern science and Greek superstition agree that this was a formless condition outside space and time, for space is determined as the distance between points, and if those points do not exist neither can space. Time is the relative movement of items within that space, so without space we cannot have time.

Perfect chaos is itself a degenerative state because random alignments of matter eventually, by pure chance, create order, just as an infinite number of monkeys with typewriters and infinite time will eventually produce the complete works of Shakespeare.

Who knows how many times great gods were created and eventually fell back into chaos before a random roll of the dice produced Eros? Eros was the greatest of the early gods for he embodied the reproductive force – the power by which the first gods could make more gods. Once that happened there began the slow disorderly process of turning chaos into cosmos (*cosmos* being the Greek word for 'order'). And when we get right down to it, that is the essence of the Greek gods – the forces of order and reason locked, then and now, in battle with the powers of chaos, unreason and entropy.

For a description of what happened next, we turn to the poet Hesiod, whose poem the *Theogony* gives us a snapshot of what the Greeks of the Archaic era (i.e. the period from 850 to 500 BC) considered to be the origins of their gods. Because Greek and Roman religion was a fluid system of belief, Hesiod's cosmogony (the study of the origins of the universe) was adapted to the conditions of succeeding centuries. And since the *Theogony* was neither canonical nor the Word of God, the people of the classical era had no inhibitions about altering Hesiod's work to fit their circumstances.

Perhaps the most dramatic change affected Eros himself, who goes from the mighty being who brought about the world as we know it to Cupid, the cuddly son of Venus, who today simpers at us from a thousand Valentine's Day cards. As Eros, the god remains the powerful reproductive force behind all things erotic as he was in the days when Gaia, the earth, was producing the ancestors of the great gods and goddesses of Greece and Rome.

Eros did not emerge from chaos alone. Erebus and Nyx, the elements of Darkness and Night respectively, combined under the influence of Eros to produce Aether and Hemera, who rebelled to become the opposite of their parents as Brightness and Day. Chaos also gave birth to Gaia who divided, amoeba-fashion, into Gaia, the earth, and Uranus, the sky. Thereafter, the earth being female and the sky male, the pair buckled down to producing further offspring heterosexually. (The Greek for 'sky' is *ouranos*, usually written today as Uranus, while his Roman counterpart is Caelus.)

At this point things get messy if we consider the Greek and Roman gods simply as super-human beings who are expected to conform to human standards of morality. The ancients were unbothered by this, since the interaction of forces is a simple physical process. Although Gaia and Uranus were in a sense equals, their offspring happily reproduced through brother-sister incest, father-daughter incest and almost any other combination of family union that one can – or would prefer not to – imagine. Yet the gods had many aspects, and at this point they did not even have a human aspect, since there were no humans yet in existence. So, saying that the earth and sky produced the next generation of gods is no more incestuous than saying that water vapour and cold combine to produce snow.

The Titans

Young Gaia, the early earth, was remarkably fecund, producing among other offspring the twelve Titans, some of whom remain familiar to us today. There is Themis, the lady of divine and natural law, who used a bronze sword to separate truth from untruth and carried a set of scales upon which to balance stronger against weaker arguments. Even today her statue is often present at courts of justice, though modern sculptors often add a blindfold to show that she is influenced by nothing other than the facts on hand.

Then there is Mnemosyne, a crucial goddess because she embodies memory, both personal and societal – every library and every textbook are within her domain. The world has been made a great deal more bearable by her daughters, those patron goddesses of the arts and science the Muses, who have a special shrine in which their own form of memory is embodied, namely the Museum.

Another Titan worthy of mention is Hyperion, the father of Eos, the dawn, and Helios, the sun. The most significant thing about Hyperion is his total lack of interest in humanity and its activities. Hyperion is not the 'god' of anything and he had no worshipers. He appears to serve only as a demonstration that the early Titans existed apart from humanity and some never really bothered themselves with that irritating new species.

Perhaps the most significant of the first generation of Titans was Cronus, the mummy's boy who was the last-born of the Titans. Cronus embodies the force of creative destruction – the force that turns a corpse into life-giving compost and uses the decay of autumn to fertilize the coming spring. His symbol is the sickle, for as the sheaves are cut down in the field the grain itself fuels life elsewhere. The Romans knew him as Saturn, an ambivalent figure who was also the god of the harvest.

Gaia had other children, including the Brontes, the craftsman race of the one-eyed Cyclopes and the 'Hundred Handed Ones', the Hecatoncheires. Uranus, with considerable justification, decided that these latter offspring were too anarchic and destructive for comfort and he had them imprisoned in Tartarus, thus setting the precedent for that gloomy place to serve as a sort of dungeon for those forces and persons deemed a threat to the cosmos.

The imprisonment of her children deeply offended Gaia, who prevailed upon her favourite son Cronus to overpower his father, use his sickle to castrate him and throw the testicles into the sea. Yet as the force of creative destruction, even as he inflicted that

Mosaic, probably depicting
Mnemosyne, from the Villa
of Els Munts, Tarraco,
1st century AD.

—

This figure has been identified
as Mnemosyne, Titaness and
mother of the nine Muses, as
the mosaic was found near
depictions of Euterpe and
Thalia, two of her daughters.

destructive act Cronus created new gods. The blood from his
violent deed spilled on the earth to create the Furies, those grim
maidens who administer their ghastly form of justice upon those
who commit ghastly crimes – particularly by children against
their parents. The Furies immediately got on to Cronus as their
first case. By his act, Cronus also inadvertently fertilized the
sea and from the foam arose the oldest of the Olympian gods,
Aphrodite, whom the Romans knew as Venus.

The wounded and literally impotent Uranus withdrew to
the heavens where he today remains as the planet of that name,
with the odd distinction of retaining his original Greek name
whereas all the other planets bear the Romanized versions of
their names, from Sol-hugging Mercury all the way out to now
dispossessed Pluto.

Cronus set himself up in his father's place and took as his
consort Rhea, a sister Titan. Rhea was worshiped by the Romans
as the Great Mother (Magna Mater) and it is no coincidence
that the founders of Rome, Romulus and Remus, had a mother
called Rhea Silvia. ('Silvia' comes from *silva*, the Latin word for
'forest', and the original Rhea's symbols were the fir tree and the
lion.) From Rhea and Cronus came the next generation of gods,
those whom humanity were to refer to as 'The Olympians'.

FIRST-GENERATION OLYMPIANS

Zeus ⋉ Jupiter

Hera ⋉ Juno

Aphrodite ⋉ Venus

Hades ⋉ Pluto

Poseidon ⋉ Neptune

Demeter ⋉ Ceres

ZEUS

⋈

JUPITER

Zeus, divinity embodied, mighty for ever, eternal king…
dealer of justice to the children of Heaven… You are enthroned
on high to watch over the rulers of cities.

Callimachus, *Ode to Zeus*

What does it take to be king of the gods? For the logical Greeks and for the even more logical Romans, a god who keeps order in the cosmos needs to be the god of order, and putting aside his many subordinate aspects, that is the main job of the god known as Zeus, Jupiter, Djeus, Diespater and Iove.

When we look at the ancient origin of these names a certain pattern begins to emerge. 'Jupiter' and 'Zeus' both seem to come from the Indo-European proto-language that was spoken around 10,000 years ago by peoples of Eurasia. 'Dius' is the daytime sky in Indo-European, and 'piter' is father, often written as 'pater'. In short, we have a 'sky-father', a concept still familiar today to those accustomed to addressing 'Our Father who art in heaven'.

Therefore, whether in the form 'Dius-Pater', who became 'Jupiter', or 'Djeus-phater', who became Zeus, this being is essentially the same god – a god who roiled the sky in thunderstorms and whose mighty weapon was the thunderbolt. In short, the sort of deity who would make a considerable impression on prehistoric agricultural peoples. Zeus/Jupiter might be a god of order, but the ancients knew that nothing maintains order better than a well-aimed thunderbolt.

Marble head of Jupiter, Roman, c. 50–200 AD.

—

Zeus and Jupiter are usually depicted as a man in mid-to-late middle age, bearded and with the serious expression expected of the being who runs the universe. This (partially restored) marble head of Jupiter is from second-century Rome, as evidenced by the hairstyle and the cut of the beard, both executed in the meticulous style of contemporary statuary.

First-Generation Olympians

We do not know the origin story of Jupiter, or indeed if the ancient Italic peoples ever gave him one. By the time Jupiter comes into the historical record he had already been merged in the minds of his followers with Zeus, whose origin story he now shared. However, Jupiter did keep one distinction – the original Roman Jupiter was a god who brought victory (though Victory herself was a separate entity called 'Victoria' by the Romans), which is why the Romans marched to war under Jupiter's symbolic bird, the eagle. Zeus was not a particularly warlike god, and for the Greeks – or at least for the ancient Athenians – the god who brought victory was Athena, who is often depicted holding Nike (the Greek embodiment of Victory) in the palm of her hand (see p. 12).

The origin story of Zeus gives us clues as to how he came to be adopted as the top god in Greece, and this in turn gives us a way of seeing how real events were translated into the Greek and Roman myths that seem so bizarre today.

Zeus' father Cronus, king of the gods (temporarily), was not unlike his father Uranus. Once in power he deeply disappointed his mother Gaia by keeping her more unruly offspring securely locked down in Tartarus. Cronus was also very well aware that he had aroused the indignation of the Furies, who had been created by his brutal act of succession. Knowing that he was therefore fated to be overthrown by his son, Cronus took to swallowing each of his children as they were born. This certainly explains why Cronus swallowed his sons Hades and Poseidon but not why he likewise swallowed his daughters Hestia, Demeter and Hera. One rather poetic explanation is that Cronus, the father of Zeus, is often identified as the god of time (which brings us back to the point discussed earlier that order emerges from time) and of course time eventually swallows all of his children, be they men or goddesses.

Chronologically, the last-born child of Rhea and her husband was Zeus, and by that time the exasperated Rhea was done with the idea of serving up her children to her spouse. When she gave birth to Zeus she substituted an appropriately sized stone, which Cronus gulped down immediately, and evidently without chewing. The newborn Zeus was smuggled away to safety.

There are a number of variations to the tale of Zeus' early years but it is generally agreed that he spent them on the island of Crete. By one Roman account, he spent those first years suspended in a cradle from a tree and was thus out of the vision of Cronus, who could see only all that was on earth or in the sea or sky. This must have been something of a challenge for

Giulia Lama, *Saturn Devouring his Child*, 18th century.

—

While mythology says that Saturn/Cronus swallowed his children whole, painters have depicted more gruesome cannibalistic feasts.

Zeus' nurse, since she was a goat called Amalthea (literally the 'nurturing goddess'), who later had Zeus transferred to a cave – this being 'in' rather than 'on' the earth and so still invisible to Cronus.

One pleasing aspect of Greek and Roman mythology is that things generally did not happen 'long ago and far away' but 'on this date, by that landmark over there'. So those wanting to visit the nursery of Zeus while on Crete can choose between two rival claimants for the site: Mount Ida, the tallest mountain on the island, or a rather gloomy cavern in the hills above the village of Psychro.

As he grew older Zeus formed an alliance with Metis, the Titan-daughter of Oceanus who embodied the concepts of planning, cunning and wisdom. Metis contrived to feed Cronus an emetic which forced him to regurgitate all his cannibalized children. While Metis was working on this aspect of the plot, Zeus entered the prison-world of Tartarus, where he successfully freed the imprisoned Cyclopes, thus earning the lasting gratitude of his grandmother, Gaia. The Cyclopes were equally grateful and equipped Zeus with the thunderbolts that were ever afterwards his primary weapon.

right

**Naucratis Painter,
black-figure kylix with Zeus
and eagle, Greek, c. 550 BC.**

–

The interior bowl of this
painted cup is attributed to
a Peloponnesian artist called
the Naucratis painter, as some
of his work was found at the
Greek trading port of that name
in Egypt. The severely archaic
style of this kylix shows Zeus on
his throne with his iconic bird,
the eagle, before him. Note the
richly embroidered robe and
Zeus' long hair braided in the
Spartan style.

opposite

**Votive slab with Jupiter
Dolichenus, Roman,
4th century AD.**

–

This triangular votive slab
from Hungary shows Jupiter
dressed as a Roman general
clutching a thunderbolt in his
left hand. The king of the gods
is posed above a sacrificial
bull (altar on the right), while
Diana (identified by her symbol
of the crescent moon) and
Apollo watch from above and
Hercules, with his club, and
Juno are shown below. The axe
shows that this is a depiction of
Jupiter Dolichenus, named after
Doliche, a city in Roman Syria.

Some tellings of the myths considered that there were
only a limited number of thunderbolts in Zeus' arsenal, but
these projectiles were more like spears than high explosives.
The Roman poets Ovid, Horace and Virgil all comment that
used thunderbolts were retrieved by the sacred bird of Zeus
and returned to heaven for further deployment. As a further
historical addendum, we note that the founding fathers of the
United States were men well steeped in the symbolism of myth,
and it is no coincidence that the great seal of the USA depicts an
eagle with a clutch of arrows in one talon.

The Romans also kept an eye out for eagles at imperial
funerals, as it was believed that an emperor's spirit was carried
to heaven by one of Jupiter's eagles. (A suspicious mind might
believe that a caged eagle was kept handy for release at the
strategic moment.)

Thus equipped with his thunderbolts and strengthened by
the return of his siblings, Zeus went to war with Cronus and
the other Titans in a struggle for domination of the Universe.
Many tales are told of this war, and as might be expected of such
a primordial struggle these accounts do not always agree, but
the upshot was clear – Zeus and his siblings were triumphant
and Cronus and his allies were imprisoned in Tartarus, with the
exception of Atlas, one of the Titan leaders, who was punished
by being forced to forever hold the heavens on his shoulders
(a job he has been doing for so long that he fossilized into the
Atlas mountain range in North Africa).

It is possible to see in the story of this fantastical struggle a more real conflict that took place in prehistoric Greece. One can imagine worship of a pre-Olympian pantheon of gods, of whom Cronus was the foremost, being slowly supplanted by the worship of new gods from Crete, an island that in Minoan times was easily ahead of mainland Greece in culture and possibly in theological sophistication.

The Romans, who were very patriarchal, were distinctly uncomfortable with how Zeus came to power, and the few Roman versions of this myth pass quickly over the subject of filial disobedience and move on to the more comfortable topic of post-war settlement, in which power was divided among the siblings.

While Romans and Greeks might not see eye-to-eye on filial rebellion, they presented a united front on the topic of misogyny. Gaia, the earth, was shared by all and under the control of none, but of her six grandchildren the three male gods took domination of the cosmos for themselves. Zeus took the sky, Poseidon the sea and Hades the underworld. Of the sisters Hestia got dominion over the household hearth, Demeter became goddess of the corn and Hera got the unenviable position of wife to Zeus.

This position had become vacant because Zeus and Metis' relationship had hit a rough patch when she became pregnant

Marble sarcophagus with Athena, Zeus and Hera and the contest between the Muses and the Sirens, Roman, 3rd century AD.
—
This sarcophagus shows Zeus as the judge in a musical contest between the nine Muses and the three Sirens. Zeus is seated with Athena (helmeted) and Hera (with diadem) beside him. The Muses from left to right include Clio (trumpet), Erato (zither), Urania (with the globe between her feet), Polyhymnia and Melpomene (with lyres, Melpomene has a theatrical mask under her feet). The Sirens, collapsing on the right, seem to be losing the contest while another Muse, Terpsichore, attempts to support a Siren in her arms – the Sirens were her daughters, after all.

with his child. Fearing that this child might supplant him, the ungrateful Zeus took the family tradition a step further and swallowed not merely the child, but the pregnant mother. (Or if we take an anthropological view, the overlap of aspects of Metis and Zeus – cunning, forward planning and so on, meant that eventually Zeus took over those functions in the rituals of pre-Archaic worshippers in early Greece.) Zeus then tried at least two other consorts before settling on the unfortunate Hera.

We shall later come to the further ramifications of the swallowing of Metis, but one immediate consequence was a distinct cooling of relations between Zeus and Prometheus, the son of Metis. Partly to spite the great king of the gods, Prometheus unilaterally decided to create a new order of beings from clay, and so arose the race of humans. Humanity was originally one large bachelor party, for Prometheus made his beings exclusively male. Distressed by the lack of culture in his new creation, the friendly Titan decided to speed up the process of civilization by stealing fire from heaven and gifting it to mankind.

The furious Zeus punished Prometheus for his theft by having him chained to a rock and then sent an eagle to consume the liver of the imprisoned Titan – an ongoing daily torture, for the liver re-grew overnight. For mankind, Zeus prepared an even more diabolical punishment – woman.

Pandora herself was quite literally gifted (Pandora means 'all gifts') with beauty, talent and an enquiring mind but also with a physical gift in the form of a large urn which she was ordered never to open. This urn was something of a time-bomb, for Zeus knew that Pandora would eventually be driven by her gods-given curiosity to open the thing. When she did so, all the troubles of the world – everything from old age and sickness to envy and hate – came swarming out before the startled girl could slam shut the lid. Only one creature was trapped behind and that one Pandora eventually made into a friend of humanity – which is why today we might have urban blight and climate change among our troubles but we also, thanks to Pandora, have Hope.

Even beset with the troubles inflicted by the gods, the earth was still swarming with humans, most of whom had adopted the worst traits of the gods and invented a few vices of their own. A frustrated Zeus decided to eliminate the entire species and sent a massive flood to wipe out mankind.

The plan came close to succeeding, but even chained to his mountain top Prometheus was able to give warning to his son Deucalion. According to the Roman writer Lucian, Deucalion and his human wife Pyrrha promptly built a large vessel on which they and selected pairs of animals rode out the flood until the receding waters eventually grounded the boat on Mount Athos in northern Greece. (Others in the Middle East, Thessaly and Sicily have also claimed their favourite mountains as the landing spot.) Soon the earth was repopulated and Zeus, aware that the king of the gods was as subject to the decrees of fate as was the humblest of living creatures, accepted the inevitable. Humanity was here to stay.

above
Pinturicchio,
The Rape of Europa, from the ceiling of the Palace of Pandolfo Petrucci, Siena, c. 1509.

opposite
Pietro Paoletti,
The Rape of Europa, from the Villa Torlonia, Rome, 19th century.

–

In this context 'rape' means an abduction or carrying away (from the same root as 'rapture').

First-Generation Olympians

In any case, Zeus had developed a new interest in a specific sub-set of humanity – beautiful princesses. Previously, Zeus' extra-marital interests had focused upon a group of female supernatural beings known as nymphs, the seduction of whom was something of a preoccupation among the male gods (to the extent that the nymphs' participation – often forced and unwilling as it was – has, nevertheless, inspired the term 'nymphomania').

Among the first of Zeus' mortal targets was Io. She was transformed into a heifer and then tormented by a vicious gadfly sent by Hera, who early perfected the art of blaming the victim. Eventually Io was driven into Asia Minor at the point known thereafter as the 'ox-crossing' (Bosphorus). Eventually she ended up in Egypt and married the Egyptian king, which for a mortal entangled in the affairs of the gods counts as a happy ending. However, Io has never fully escaped her seducer, for she is now a moon, endlessly circling the planet Jupiter.

A Phoenician princess called Europa also encountered Zeus, who this time took the bovine form himself (Zeus tried out other guises for his seductions, including a ram, a swan and an ant). In the form of a bull Zeus carried his abductee – it is uncertain how enthusiastic the princess was about all this – westwards where she eventually became a continent (Europe) and also a moon of Jupiter, and the mother of King

Minos of Crete. We note again the connection with Crete and the central role of the bull in Cretan religion, which we will see once more in the legend of the Minotaur.

The romantic liaisons of Zeus are too numerous to detail here, but we can note that his claim to be the Sky Father was quite literally true in the case of numerous minor deities, including the nine Muses, the three Graces, Persephone and Hebe, goddess of youth.

Of the later Olympian gods Zeus fathered Hermes/Mercury with Maia, a daughter of Atlas, then Apollo and Artemis/Diana with Leto, a Titan, and Dionysus/Bacchus with the mortal Semele. Since Zeus and Hera made both love and war it is logical that one fruit of their union was Ares/Mars, the god of war. Another child was Eris, known to the Romans as 'Discordia'.

Thus by the most common accounting of the twelve Olympian gods we have Aphrodite, the eldest, four of the siblings of Zeus and six of his children. The obliging Hestia stepped down from the divine pantheon when Dionysus came on the scene, and Hades was not conventionally numbered among the Olympians. There were twelve Olympians because the numbers twelve (divisible by most other numbers) and seven (a prime number) were considered especially significant. Even today we might consider the twelve disciples and the twelve signs of the Zodiac – in both European and Chinese astrology.

Having stocked the heavens with gods, Zeus proceeded to stock the earth with heroes. Among his most notable offspring we find, in chronological order: Perseus, Heracles, Castor and Pollux – also known as Gemini, the twins – and Helen of Troy.

Such a profusion of illegitimate children may seem to somewhat tarnish Zeus in his capacity as the god of order, but this is because we look at matters from a modern moral viewpoint. From an ancient perspective the point of fidelity within marriage was to keep track of parentage rather than have the couple remain faithful to one another. The bridegroom certainly did not commit to 'forswearing all others', and he was not expected to. The point of children within marriage was to keep property within the family by having a next generation to pass it on to. While it was usually pretty clear who a child's mother was, one could only be sure of the father if the mother had one exclusive sex partner. A mother's infidelity broke the bloodline, which was bad; a father's infidelity spread it around, which bothered no one very much.

Furthermore, it was not merely the job of Zeus/Jupiter to maintain order, he had to wrest it from chaos. Zeus begot not

Fresco with Leda and Zeus in the form of a swan, Pompeii, 1st century AD.

–

This fresco depicts another transformation of Zeus – this time into a swan. This was part of his seduction of Leda of Sparta, a union in which Helen of Troy was conceived. The fresco was discovered in 2018 after painstaking excavations of a bedroom in Pompeii, which had been buried for centuries.

merely children, but much-needed allies, because there was a lot of chaos to be dealt with. For example, all of Zeus' divine children had to club together (literally) to defeat the race of giants when these monstrous beings decided it was their turn to rule from Olympus. This resulted in a massive struggle known as the Gigantomachy and who did what in this war did much to decide the relative status of the junior Olympians.

Another challenge faced by Zeus and family was the monstrous Typhon, a creature of hideous strength, who nearly defeated the combined power of the gods. While Typhon was eventually confined to Tartarus, the numerous monsters that he spawned continued to wreak havoc across the earth. This time it was the job of the heroes to tidy up, and while the early heroes of myth were far from clean-living examples to ancient youth, they did a splendid job of fighting the forces of chaos and unreason and in so doing made the earth safer for future generations.

Zeus had several aspects, most of which were associated with his dual roles as a weather god and the god of order. Thus we

opposite left
Fresco with Zeus, from the House of the Dioscuri, Pompeii, 1st century AD.

—

This fresco shows Zeus seated in all his pomp, being crowned by the goddess Victory (Nike). His iconic eagle is at his feet, along with the globe (the Romans were well aware that the Earth was a sphere). It is possible that this illustration was based upon the statue of Zeus at Olympia (see p.13)

opposite right
Giovanni Battista Tiepolo, fresco with Jupiter, from the Room of Olympus, Villa Valmarana ai Nani, Vicenza, 1757.

—

Jupiter, again with his iconic eagle, sits on the clouds as if sitting on a more solid throne.

see Zeus worshiped specifically as the god of the markets – as in orderly fair trade in opposition to his son Hermes, the anarchic deceiver. Likewise in maintaining a well-regulated society Zeus was the guardian of oaths and the god of hospitality. (One host who mistreated his guests was Lycus, a king whose misdeeds got him transformed by Zeus into the first werewolf.)

As might be expected of the king of the gods, temples to Zeus were splendid and abundant. Often these temples honoured Zeus in his role as patron-protector of a particular city, such as the epic temple of Zeus in Athens. While this temple contained a massive statue of the god, it was far surpassed in fame by the statue of Zeus in his temple at Olympia, which was one of the wonders of the ancient world. (While Mount Olympus, home of the gods, is in northern Greece, Olympia was in the Peloponnesian state of Elis. Thus we get the name of the Olympian gods from the mountain, while the Olympic Games get their name from the Peloponnesian site.)

Perhaps the most splendid of all temples to the king of the gods was in Rome, where the Temple of Iuppiter Optimus Maximus (Jupiter the best and greatest) dominated the Capitoline Hill. One reason this temple was so splendid was because, as Rome grew wealthier and more powerful, Jupiter incinerated earlier versions of his temple with well-placed lightning bolts, thus forcing the Romans each time to build a new edifice more in keeping with the god's increased standing. Jupiter shared the premises with Juno and Minerva; together, the Romans called the three gods the Capitoline Triad.

After four rebuildings the Romans produced something satisfactory – a building of jaw-dropping splendour. Plutarch tells us the roof was made of gilded bronze and the temple contained some of the finest statuary in the known world. Many of Rome's most important rituals, from the swearing-in of the consuls to the endpoint of a Roman triumph, featured this temple.

Yet the splendid Capitoline temple, and the other temples to Jupiter and Zeus, are either long gone or now in ruins. Still, there is a better way, even today, to commune with the king of the gods should you so wish. Proceed to Dodona in north-western Greece, from where the first of the race of Hellenes originated. Here you will find a grove of oak trees which have been sacred to Zeus for well over three thousand years. There in that grove one can do as the priests of centuries ago once did – remove your footwear to touch the ground directly, and listen for the voice of Zeus whispering in the leaves in this most ancient of oracles.

HERA
⋈
JUNO

Hera, whom they call the revered nurse of the Graces,
who is said to wield sovereignty and hold the sceptre.

Colluthus, *Abduction of Helen* 86

If, as many scholars now believe, Zeus was one of a new generation of gods whose worship spread from Crete through mainland Greece, then one way to make the newcomer acceptable to the local people would have been to 'marry' him to an existing goddess. This is what seems to have happened in the case of Zeus and Hera, since Hera and Poseidon are perhaps the original Olympians – gods whose worship was always native to Greece. For this opinion we have the authority of Herodotus who wrote 2,500 years ago:

> *My enquiries have convinced me that the names of the gods are imported from abroad, and I believe that they mostly came from Egypt. Except for Poseidon... Hera, Hestia and Themis... the other names were always in use in Egypt.*
> Herodotus, *Histories*, 2.50

Herodotus should know, for his name means 'the gift of the Lady' – because whatever Hera's name or where she came from, we don't really know what she called herself. 'Hera' simply means something analogous to 'Lady', just as the masculine form of 'hera' is 'hero' – which in Homeric times

Hera Farnese, Roman copy of Greek original (from 5th century BC), 1st century AD.
—
Hera wears a light indoor Greek chiton and a diadem of rank atop her elegant coiffure. (In antiquity elaborate female hairstyles were a signal of high status.) Hera's raised arm and extended index finger show her in the *adlocutio* pose, usually used to depict persons of authority addressing a public gathering.

First-Generation Olympians

Attributed to the Brygos
Painter, two red-figure
lekythoi with Hera, Greek,
left: c. 490–480 BC;
right: c. 500–475 BC.

–

The goddess is recognizable
by her distinctive lotus-tipped
staff, the narrow cloth band
around her head – called a
fillet – which symbolized royalty,
and the cuckoo, which is one of
her iconic birds. (The other is a
peacock.) Hera is wearing a rich
version of the contemporary
Ionic chiton.

(*c.* 1000–800 BC) meant the leader of a large war-band who might or might not have been heroic. So 'Hera' is a title rather than a name.

In any case, ox-eyed Hera, the Lady, the golden goddess of the starry night, was married early on to the usurper god Zeus in a union that – like most marriages in the ancient world – had a lot more to do with convenience than love. If the union of Zeus and Hera came about by Zeus displacing his predecessors and pairing with Hera, we might expect to see the actual events reflected in the Greek myths, and indeed we do. The cuckoo is infamous for kicking other fledglings out of the nest and enjoying the sole attention of the mother. So according to myth, Zeus disguised himself as a distressed cuckoo in need of care. When Hera took the bird into her arms in a moment of uncharacteristic soft-heartedness, Zeus returned to his normal form and ravished her, marrying her afterwards.

Thus Hera came to be the wife of Zeus and in time she became conflated with Juno of the Romans. However, the merging of these two goddesses was far from seamless, for while Jupiter and Zeus were largely similar figures, Juno and Hera had some quite significant differences to reconcile. For a start it is quite possible that – as a mirror image to Zeus and Hera – it was Jupiter who was always native to the Latin peoples who founded Rome, and Juno was the one who was imported (as a result of Rome's long and complex history with the Etruscans).

In some of her original attributes Juno was closer to Athena than Hera, for both Athena and Juno were once war-goddesses with goat-skin armour. Hera was less warlike, though she put up a good showing in the war with the Giants. However, she was later wounded by Heracles, and in the Trojan War she was more keen on politics than fighting. Also, while both Juno and Hera were goddesses of marriage – which is why even today *June* is the favoured month for weddings – by common agreement Hera was something of a rotten parent while Juno was the mother of the entire Roman state and later empire. One could say that the major difference between Juno and Hera is that Hera was a wife and Juno was a mother.

An example of Juno as the mothering protector of Rome comes early in the city's history when Gallic invaders attempted to catch unawares the guards on Rome's Capitoline Hill. The sneak attack was foiled when the sacred geese of Juno started hissing – and even today those farms with geese have little need for a watchdog. As a result of her intervention Juno gained the further epithet of *Moneta* – 'she who gives warning'. We live with one consequence of this in modern times, for in later years the Roman mint was located in the temple of Juno Moneta and the coins which were produced there were 'money'.

Nevertheless, despite her distinct history and her far greater role in the rituals of the Roman state, the complex goddess Juno eventually became Hera, a goddess who is essentially defined by her role as the spouse of Zeus. As a repeatedly wronged wife Hera becomes the villain of many of the myths because, unable to strike at her husband, she largely aimed her vindictiveness at Zeus' sexual partners and illegitimate offspring.

For example, Hera once sent a gadfly to torment the unfortunate Io while she was transformed into a white heifer. Zeus had effected the transformation to hide his lover from Hera upon her unexpected appearance, and Hera was immediately deeply suspicious of the animal. Therefore she asked Zeus to give it to her as a gift. Zeus could hardly refuse without giving the game away, so Hera took away her prisoner and had her watched over by hundred-eyed Argus.

Zeus enlisted the wily Hermes to kill Argus and so free Io, whereupon Hera unleashed the gadfly. As a gesture to the watchman who had died in her service, Hera moved his eyes to the tails of the first peacocks, and along with the cuckoo (for obvious reasons), the peacock has been the symbolic bird of Hera ever since, just as the eagle stands in for Zeus and the owl for Athena.

Many of the stories concerning Hera deal with her savage treatment of the lovers of Zeus, which is all the more unfair

opposite
Detail of a tapestry with Juno, Brussels, *c.* 1520–30.
–
Juno, imagined as a battle queen, is seen here in one of three extant panels of a tapestry woven for King John III of Portugal (r. 1521–1557).

left & right
Scenes from the myth of Juno, Argus and Io, from composite codex for Raphael de Mercatellis, *c.* 1500.
–
These codex illustrations show Juno entrusting the nymph Io (disguised as a heifer) to the guardianship of hundred-eyed Argus. In the next scene Mercury charms Argus to sleep and kills him. After Argus failed in his task his eyes were transferred to the tails of Hera's iconic peacocks.

because many of these lovers were coerced or deceived by Zeus in the first place. It is also a sad commentary on Greco-Roman life that the mythological behaviour of Hera reflected the actual conduct of many wives who brutally punished slave-girls who had no choice but to submit to their master's advances. Whether goddess or Greek or Roman woman, a wife could not punish her husband for infidelity, so she took it out on his victim. Or as a Roman proverb put it, 'If you can't beat the donkey, you hit the saddle'.

The most famous case is Hera's bitter persecution of Heracles, the son of Zeus and Alcmene, despite the fact that the hero's name itself represents a futile attempt to appease the goddess (Heracles means 'glory of Hera').

At one point Athena tried to arouse some maternal tenderness in Hera by putting the infant Heracles at her breast while she was sleeping. The cunning plan worked at first, but then the vigour with which the babe pulled at her teat informed Hera exactly who was doing the suckling. At this realization Hera jerked the child from her breast so violently that the milk Heracles was sucking sprayed right across the sky, where it remains today as the Milky Way. Add an attempt to kill baby Heracles by dropping venomous snakes next to his cradle and sending the goddess Lyssa to drive the adult Heracles temporarily mad, and we see an unhealthy tendency for vendetta to become something of a full-scale obsession.

Hera's disputes with her husband went further than exasperation at his infidelities, but she always had to tread carefully when dealing with the king of the gods. (It should be noted that Hera is in no way the 'queen of the gods' – her position was dependent entirely on Zeus and she had no authority otherwise.) In the *Iliad*, Zeus casually and frequently threatens his wife with violence and Hera responds with tactics familiar to sociologists who deal with spousal abuse today – verbal deflection and aggression, appeasement, moral pressure and an attempt to engage allies. We also see her son Hephaestus reacting exactly as might a child today in similar circumstances. 'Endure it [his behaviour] please mother… for you are dear to me and I can't watch while he strikes you in front of me, and even though it grieves me, I am unable to defend you.'

In one case when Zeus was becoming altogether too arbitrary and autocratic, Hera even attempted to orchestrate a coup in conjunction with the other gods. This failed catastrophically and Hera ended up suspended from the clouds by her wrists with

Tintoretto (Robusti Jacopo), *The Origin of the Milky Way*, c. 1575.

—

After the baby Heracles was wrenched from her nipple, milk from Hera's breast sprayed across the heavens to form the 'Milky Way'. Note that the artist has included the eagle of Zeus and the peacock of Hera in this work. Though otherwise naked, Hera still wears her royal tiara.

anvils tied to her ankles. Yet in this case Zeus realized that his wife had a point and moderated his behaviour thereafter.

Indeed, Zeus often complained that his wife got away with behaviour he would not accept from any other god. 'I don't get as angry with her [as with the others] because I'm used to her trying to subvert anything I plan,' he remarks at one point, adding that she 'provokes me with abusive words. Forever among the immortal gods she fights against me.'

Occasionally others were caught in the crossfire between husband and wife. When the mortal Tiresias offended Hera, she transformed him into a woman for seven years. Restored to masculinity, he was asked to resolve a dispute between Zeus and Hera: having experienced sex from the viewpoint of both genders, for whom was it most pleasurable? Tiresias replied that the woman got nine-tenths of the fun, an answer that so angered Hera that she struck Tiresias blind. One basic law of the cosmos was that one god could not undo another's actions, so Zeus had to compensate by giving Tiresias the gift of prophecy and extending his lifetime to seven times the usual mortal span.

While the infidelities of Zeus were many, as the protector of marriage Hera had little choice but to remain true to her spouse. It is also true that, given who her spouse was, there were very few who were brave enough to tempt her to stray. One who did was a particularly obnoxious specimen called Ixion, king of the Lapiths. Ixion was a grandchild of Zeus (through being a son of Ares), and this is probably what saved him when he violated the rules of guest-friendship and family decorum by pushing his father-in-law to a grisly death in a pit of red-hot coals.

Deservedly exiled from his native city, Ixion lived as an outcast until Zeus gave him sanctuary on Olympus. By way of returning the favour Ixion set about seducing Hera, the wife of Zeus – and his grandmother. Zeus quickly noticed what was going on and sculpted a cloud into the form of Hera, and upon this Ixion consummated his lust. (The seed falling through the cloud created the first of the race of centaurs.) Immediately afterwards Ixion was blasted from the heavens by a fiery thunderbolt and followed to earth by Hermes, who bound Ixion to a wheel of

Giulio Romano, *Psyche Appealing in Vain to Juno*, Palazzo del Te, Mantua, *c.* 1526–28.
—
This painting shows a scene from a Roman 2nd-century novel, *The Golden Ass* by Apuleius. Here Psyche, the protagonist of one of the stories, appeals (unsuccessfully) to Juno for succour.

First-Generation Olympians

Juno, from the manuscript
Ovide moralisé, c. 1380–90.

—

Juno looks particularly queenly
in this manuscript illumination.
Ovide moralisé retold and
reinterpreted tales from Ovid's
Metamorphoses for a medieval
Christian audience.

fire. Ixion might have protested that Zeus felt less strongly
about husbandly rights when he was seducing Alcmene, wife of
Amphitryon and mother of Heracles, but to no avail. Somewhere
in Tartarus Ixion is still bound on that wheel and bound to Zeus'
double standard, doomed to spin until the cosmos comes to
an end.

Ixion had reason to be interested in Hera, who is described
as both regal and attractive – she did after all dispute with
Aphrodite and Athena for the title of 'the fairest'. She is often
referred to in poetry as 'white-armed' and 'ox-eyed', the latter
apparently being a compliment among ancient Greeks. Knowing
her husband's fetish for virgins she annually bathed in a sacred
stream near the city of Argos – of which she was patron and
protector – to renew her maidenhood.

Apart from in Argos, worship of Hera was widespread
throughout the Peloponnese, and she was particularly honoured
in Sparta and the city of Elis. The Olympics were held every
four years in Elis and between celebrations of this major event
another was held in honour of Hera, in which only female
athletes competed.

left

Detail of Juno, from a fresco depicting the marriage of Jupiter and Juno, House of the Tragic Poet, Pompeii, 1st century AD.

—

In this fresco Juno and Jupiter are married on Mount Ida. Juno, wearing her veil and golden jewelry, has the appearance of a typical wealthy Roman bride.

In Rome the major celebration of Juno was not an athletic event but the festival of the Matronalia, celebrating once more Juno's connection with motherhood. However, Juno also embodied most forms of the feminine in Rome. For example, women could not be guided by a creative genius, only men could, so the female equivalent was the spirit of Juno.

In his continuation of the story of the *Iliad*, the Roman poet Virgil has Juno taking up Hera's animus against the Trojans in her persecution of the hero Aeneas. After fleeing Troy Aeneas was fated to settle in Italy, where his descendants would found Rome. Juno was opposed to the idea because her favoured city was Carthage (again we see the theme of Juno as an imported goddess) and the founding of Rome inevitably entailed the later destruction of Carthage.

opposite

Giovanni Ambrogio Figino, *Jupiter, Juno and Io*, Milan, 1599.

—

This painting depicts the tense moment where Juno almost caught her husband dallying with the nymph Io – here on the right after being hastily transformed into a heifer (though the original myths insist that the heifer was milk-white).

First-Generation Olympians

APHRODITE
⚥
VENUS

Muse, now tell me the deeds of golden Aphrodite,
She from Cyprus who arouses sweet desire in the gods
Who masters the races of humanity,
And also the birds in the sky and all the creatures
Of the dry land and the sea
All those know what she of the beautiful garlands has wrought.

To Aphrodite, Homeric Hymn 5.1 1–7

According to popular belief, love is the grease that spins the world on its axis, and countless books and films teach that marriage is the ultimate destination of a romantic relationship. This was not always the case, and certainly the remorselessly practical Romans saw things differently. They believed that marriage was above all a business relationship, one that linked families and carried each family's assets on to the next generation. They conceded that love may result from a marriage, but only as a by-product and not necessarily a welcome one – the Roman jurist Gaius says that care must be taken that a young couple not fall in love lest they 'despoil one another with gifts through mutual affection'. The Roman goddess of married couples was not Venus but Cloacina, who was also the goddess of sewers (she was connected to marriage because of her close association with Juno, patron of married women).

So it is no surprise that in ancient Rome there are few signs of a love goddess of any description. When Venus did make an appearance in Rome, she did so as Venus *Obsequens*, 'Obedient Venus', she who does as others desire. Her temple was subsidized by fines levied on women found guilty of sexual misconduct. In fact, the word from which 'Venus' is derived has

Burney Relief, probably a representation of Ishtar, Old Babylonian, 19th–18th century BC.

Shown here on a large terracotta plaque, this early goddess (Ishtar/Inanna) had the role of several later Greek and Roman deities and her symbology includes lions (like Rhea) and owls (Athena).

the same root as the modern word 'venom', so nasty were love potions reckoned to be.

It was definitely a tough start for a goddess who appears to have originated, innocuously enough, among the early Latins as a minor goddess of flowers and cultivated gardens – a relationship that we maintain today whenever flowers are given to a loved one. In the eastern Mediterranean flowers were one of the symbols of the goddess Anath, who came to be merged in some Semitic religions with the goddess Astarte, which is how worship of Venus first became properly established in Rome.

This came about in 217 BC, at a time when the Romans were being comprehensively and repeatedly defeated by the Carthaginians during the Second Punic War. In desperate times the Romans would consult their oracle of last resort, the Sibylline books, and their consultation revealed that, for Rome to win, it was essential that Astarte be brought over to the Roman side. The Romans felt that this was a good idea, because despite her connection with flowers, Astarte was no delicate blossom. As well as being the goddess of sexual love, Astarte Ishtar was also a powerful war goddess – proving yet again that one can indeed simultaneously make love and war.

It has already been established that the ancients could give gods job interviews. The Romans took this further and aggressively head-hunted deities whom they felt would be beneficial to the Roman project. Astarte, whom the Romans decided was a version of Venus, was duly courted in this manner and seduced from her main temple in Eryx, Sicily, to become ensconced in Rome as Venus *Erycina.*

Venus fresco, Roman, House of Venus in the Shell, Pompeii, 1st century AD.

–

This spectacular fresco takes up the back wall of the peristyle. The subject is immediately identifiable as Venus because of the association with the sea, the Cupid lurking nearby and because Venus/Aphrodite was the only goddess whom the ancients routinely depicted in the nude.

First-Generation Olympians

At this point Venus – conspicuously absent from early Roman festivals – makes an appearance on 23 April, *Dies Meretricia* or 'Prostitute's Day'. This is when, says the poet Ovid, 'you prostitutes… give the Mistress myrtle, which she loves… and crowd the temple [of Venus Erycina] at the Colline Gate'.

With increasing exposure to the Hellenistic world – a world that the Romans realized was culturally superior to theirs in many ways – came an increased tendency to identify Venus with

Marble statue of Venus, Roman (after a Greek original c. 200 BC), c. 100–150 AD.

—

This Roman statue of Venus finishing a bath is one of numerous variations on this theme. The symbology of the vase (a receptacle) and discarded clothing are a counterpoint to the goddess's assumed modesty.

Relief showing Anchises, Aphrodite and Aeneas as a baby, from a temple in Aphrodisias, 1st century AD.
–
This relief was excavated in Aphrodisias, in south-western Anatolia. When the Roman Empire became Christian the city's name was changed from the 'pagan' goddess to Stauropolis – the 'City of the Cross'.

the Greek goddess Aphrodite. This identification was helped by the fact that in Greece Aphrodite was also worshiped as Aphrodite of the Gardens – again linking Venus, Aphrodite and Ishtar through the symbolism of flowers.

At around this time the Romans had also come to reimagine themselves as descendants of Trojans who had fled as their native city was destroyed by the Greeks – a foundation myth that was to become fully realized two centuries later in the epic *Aeneid* of Virgil. If the Trojan hero Aeneas was the literary ancestor of the Roman people, then a degree of respect had to be shown to his mother, who, according to myth, was Aphrodite/Venus.

This respect, and respectability, became evident in a more genteel temple founded in central Rome, dedicated to Venus

Genetrix, 'the mother', with the wider meaning of the word *genea* referring to a breed or bloodline. Since the Roman aristocracy were very keen on bloodlines, Venus Genetrix was much visited by the matriarchs of Rome's top families. Venus as Aphrodite was now fully established, and as a relatively obscure former vernal goddess, Venus had no origin story that needed adaptation and so she adopted wholesale Aphrodite's background.

As we have seen, the most popular of the stories of Aphrodite's origin was that she was the eldest of the Olympian gods, being born from the foam when the genitals of Uranus were tossed into the sea. The Greek for 'foam' is *aphros* and in this case the word may have arisen from the origin story, rather than the other way around. Aphrodite is by any measure a very ancient goddess.

By whatever means she was conceived, Aphrodite appears to have had no childhood, but sprang into being as a fully grown, nubile but ageless goddess possessed of irresistible sexual attraction. Unlike other goddesses, Aphrodite in the ancient

right
Aeneid Master, Venus and Juno provoke Dido's love for Aeneas, c. 1530.
—
An enamel showing a dispute between Venus, mother of Aeneas, Juno, protector of Carthage, and Dido.

Francesco del Cossa,
*Allegory of April: The
Triumph of Venus* (detail),
from the Palazzo Schifanoia,
Ferrara, 1476–84.

–

This Renaissance painting
shows the coming of spring.
Venus (centre) is towed by
swans, which symbolize fidelity.
Courting lovers and rabbits
emphasize the message of
new life and love.

world was frequently depicted in the nude – something that would be unthinkable for a goddess such as Hera, and even less for Hera's more staid Roman counterpart, Juno. It also helped Venus to transition into Roman society as Aphrodite that the Greek goddess was generally regarded favourably by the poets, who referred to her as 'golden', 'laughter-loving', 'bright' and 'celestial'. As well as love, Aphrodite embodied grace and beauty – topics about which the still somewhat rustic Romans were well aware they had much to learn.

In myth Aphrodite's rare beauty was something of a problem for Zeus – who in some alternate forms of the Aphrodite origin story was also her father through an earlier marriage to the Titan Dione. Since competition for Aphrodite's charms might cause civil war among the male gods of Olympus, Zeus was happy to see her married off to Hephaestus, though the marriage of the beautiful, outgoing Aphrodite to the lame, introverted craftsman god quickly showed that opposites can repel as well as attract.

Given the incompatibility of the pair, it is unsurprising that Aphrodite was a terrible wife who largely abandoned her workaholic spouse and instead conducted flagrant affairs with men and gods alike. The Roman Venus had certain warlike

opposite
Pinturicchio,
The Judgment of Paris,
***c.*1509.**

–

In this Renaissance ceiling panel Paris holds the golden apple in his hand and decides whether Aphrodite (left), Hera (centre) or Athena (right) is 'the fairest'.

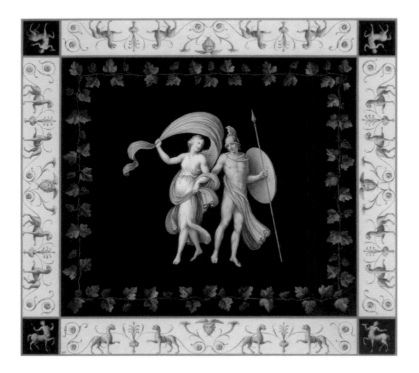

left
Ares and Aphrodite surrounded by vines, Italian, 17th century.

–

The panel by an anonymous artist shows influences of contemporary (the figures), Roman (the vines), Greek (the centaurs in the corners) and Assyrian (the lions) style.

First-Generation Olympians

characteristics and was the patron deity of generals such as Caesar and Sulla, but the closest Aphrodite came to martial vigour was her enduring relationship with the war god Ares. Her eastern counterpart Astarte/Ishtar might have been a war goddess, but Aphrodite herself was definitely a lover and not a fighter.

When the terrifying monster Typhon sought the destruction of the Olympian gods, Aphrodite fled for cover and was sheltered by the fishy Ichthyes, who disguised her as one of their own. As a reward, they were lifted to the heavens as the constellation of Pisces. When a beautiful species of ray-finned fish was discovered in 2018, classically minded researchers named it *Tosanoides Aphrodite*, in the belief that should the goddess of beauty ever take piscean form, it would look something like that.

In the Trojan War Aphrodite supported the Trojans – naturally enough, since it was the judgment of Paris crowning Aphrodite 'the fairest' that had started the war in the first place. That is, Paris was asked to decide who was more beautiful – Hera, Aphrodite or Athena – and he chose Aphrodite, who rewarded Paris with the love of the most beautiful woman on earth. This was Helen, who at the time was already married to Menelaus, the king of Sparta. When Helen eloped with Paris, her husband did not take this development well and things went downhill from there.

Aphrodite tried to help the Trojans in battle, but was wounded by the hero Diomedes and healed by the goddess Dione (who Homer reckoned to have been Aphrodite's mother). Thereafter Zeus himself confirmed what everyone knew of Aphrodite anyway, saying 'Not to you, my child is given power in war. Leave such things to Athena and Ares.'

In Greek and particularly Roman myth the goddess's henchman is usually the chubby little archer Cupid, who has thoroughly muddled origins. The Romans were relatively clear about things, claiming that Cupid was the child of Venus by either Mercury or Mars – given what they knew of Venus, they accepted that the father's identity might be uncertain.

The Greeks made things much more confusing by considering the Roman Cupid to be Eros – a god who is simultaneously the son of Aphrodite and the primordial entity who brought Aphrodite's 'father' Uranus into being (though a philosopher might argue that even this was possible, since in the very early stages of the cosmos, things like time had not yet settled down). Lovers should note, though, that both Cupid and Eros were given wings because the ancients knew well that love is not a settled condition and might easily fly off.

By the later classical era Aphrodite's hitman had a bow with two sets of arrows. One set was tipped with gold and caused instant desire, and the other set was lead-tipped and caused instant revulsion. All that Aphrodite needed to create instant tragedy was to have Cupid fire one arrow from each set at a pair of victims and stand back to watch the chaos. Apollo – whom Aphrodite seems to have cursed with a particularly unhappy love life – was an early target, doomed by Cupid to pursue the nymph Daphne, who was so repulsed by him that she had herself turned into a bush to escape him. The bush was the laurel, which was ever after sacred to Apollo (see p. 143).

Aphrodite was not immune to her own influence and she fell in lust with numerous men during her career. (Like almost all Greek and Roman goddesses, she was exclusively heterosexual.) Her affair with Ares produced the offspring Phobos (panic) and Deimos (terror), who are now moons of Mars. While Cupid is a possible son of Hermes/Mercury, Hermaphroditus was unmistakeably the child of Hermes and Aphrodite, combining the names and genders of both parents. Hermaphroditus joined Cupid and Anteros as part of Aphrodite's retinue, a group known collectively as the *erotes*, minor gods of love and sex.

Another child of Aphrodite/Venus was Priapus, a rustic god of plants and fertility who – possibly as a demonstration of

Roman mosaic showing triumph of Venus, Thuburbo Maius, 4th century AD.

—

Venus stands on a chariot being pulled by four cupids. The mosaic is made up of both floral and shell-inspired patterns, motifs strongly associated with the goddess.

warped Roman humour – was cursed by Juno to sport a massive erection until he was about to have sex, whereupon he wilted away to impotence.

Two epithets of the goddess, Aphrodite *Pandemos* and Venus *Vulgivaga* – both of which roughly translate as 'everyone's goddess' – show that love and sex are essential parts of humanity, as they must be if we are to have more humans. The influence of Aphrodite/Venus is everywhere in myth and this has passed into modern culture in sometimes unexpected ways.

For example, another of Aphrodite's lusts was for that most impossibly handsome of mortal men, young Adonis. According to the legend recounted by Ovid, Aphrodite was infuriated by the sexual abstinence of a princess called Myrrha. To avenge the rejection of all that she stood (or lay down) for, Aphrodite inflicted Myrrha with an incestuous lust for her father and Myrrha seduced him in disguise. When he discovered the identity of his nocturnal visitor, Myrrha's father was incensed, and for her protection the gods transformed Myrrha into a bush from which came her tears (myrrh) and eventually Adonis, since Myrrha's transformation evidently did not affect her pregnancy.

Adonis later died tragically in Aphrodite's arms after a hunting 'accident' (suspects who might have arranged the accident include Ares, Apollo and Artemis). The blood of Adonis mingled with Aphrodite's tears to create the anemone flower. Thus just the one myth gives the modern world a flower, a precious natural oil and a term for a very handsome man.

Aphrodite was worshiped across the Mediterranean world, and in the different forms of Astarte and Ishtar much further east as well. How Aphrodite was perceived depended on what aspects of love interested her worshipers. The somewhat staid Romans of the Republic liked her as Venus *Verticordia*, 'the turner of hearts', who showed wanton women the error of their ways. (She was also eventually merged with the goddess of marriage as Venus Cloacina.) Those worshipers of the goddess who preferred wanton women could turn to Aphrodite *Porne* – the goddess of carnal lust. Pictures of the latter's devotees in action are termed *porne graphos* – pornography.

Detail of a fresco with Hermaphroditus playing a barbiton, Capua, 2nd century AD.

–

Hermaphroditus, merged with Salmacis (see opposite), had both male and female characteristics. The instrument he holds is a barbiton, which the Greeks and Romans claimed to have a deeper, more erotic tone than the classical lyre.

First-Generation Olympians

Jan Gossaert, *The Metamorphosis of Hermaphroditus and Salmacis, c. 1520*

This painting illustrates the origin of Hermaphroditus' dual-sexed form, as told in Ovid's *Metamorphoses*.

Salmacis, an obssessive naiad (freshwater nymph), wished to be united with Hermaphroditus forever. The gods granted her desire very literally. In the background, on the left, you can see their bodies fused into one form.

HADES
⚔
PLUTO

Great king, Zeus of the underworld,
Whose dark realm lies far from mortal strife...
You hold the keys to the earth
And unlock its secret gates.

To Pluto, Orphic Hymn 17

The gods of Olympus were not the only pantheon of Greco-Roman gods. Olympus had its counterpart in the gloomy underworld kingdom of Hades, and the gods of that place were known as chthonic – 'of the earth'. Among these gods the Greeks counted Persephone, Hecate and Hermes, though the latter had a foot also in the Olympian pantheon, being a god who crosses – or transgresses – boundaries. The undisputed master of the dark kingdom was Hades, the elder brother of Zeus – pale, dark-bearded and austere, master of so many souls that he was often called *Pluton*, the 'lord of many'.

While the Romans had a more complex relationship with the lord of the underworld, to the Greeks Hades was a straightforward character. He was a son of Rhea and Cronus, and was duly gulped down by his cannibalistic father. Being the first male child to be swallowed, Hades was the last of the brothers to be vomited up when Cronus was forced to disgorge his victims – which may explain his famous lack of a sense of humour. In the war against the Titans, Hades revealed himself as a mighty warrior, and the craftsman tribe of the Cyclopes gave him thanks for his efforts, since he had freed them from Tartarus. These thanks took the form of a helmet of invisibility,

Cristofano Gherardi, *Pluto*, 1555–57.

—

This painting shows Pluto as a grey-haired god, immediately identifiable by his bident (two pronged spear) and his three-headed hound Cerberus.

which on occasion Hades would make available to various heroes for their quests.

The war against the Titans was the first and last time that Hades was involved in battle, for when the victorious brothers Zeus, Poseidon and Hades divided the cosmos between them, Hades drew the underworld. Once ensconced on his dread throne as lord of the dead, Hades thereafter paid little attention to the affairs of the living, be they mortal or divine. Not for Hades, then, the war against the Giants, and when mighty Typhon came to overthrow the gods and the rule of reason, Hades perceived his rampage only as a distant echo.

We should note, however, that Hades was lord of the dead, not the personification of death itself, a role that fell to another character called Thanatos. In fact, the two seldom had reason to meet, for Thanatos concerned himself with the (about to stop) living, and Hades was responsible for those who had already passed away.

opposite

Priamo della Quercia, miniature of Dante and Virgil being rowed across the River Styx, from *The Divine Comedy* by Dante Alighieri, 1442–50.

–

This illustration shows a scene from Dante's recently completed *Divine Comedy*.

First-Generation Olympians

opposite left

Attributed to the Diosphos Painter, amphora with Hypnos (Sleep) and Thanatos (Death) carrying Sarpedon, Greek, 5th century BC.

—

This Archaic-style vase shows the hero Sarpedon at the moment he passes from unconsciousness to death after being struck by Patroclus, the companion of Achilles, during the siege of Troy.

opposite right

Terracotta neck-amphora with Athena, Heracles, Cerberus and Hermes, Greek, c. 525–500 BC.

—

In this depiction Cerberus has two heads, facing opposite directions. While we are familiar with the three-headed version, Cerberus had anywhere between two and fifty heads according to different ancient sources.

Because the only sounds that came to him from the world above were when men uttered his name as an imprecation of a curse, Hades was not widely worshiped. Moreover, great care was taken to avoid coming to the attention of Hades, lest the lord of the dead decide to take up the relationship more personally. As a result, Hades was referred to mainly through a series of euphemisms and when it became necessary to sacrifice to him, the person doing the sacrifice did so with their face averted. Sacrifices to Hades were usually creatures with black pelts and unlike offerings to the other gods, even the flesh of the victim was burned up – a type of sacrifice called a *holocaust* ('complete burning').

Despite his grim reputation, there were those who sacrificed to Hades, one reason being that sometimes it was necessary to sacrifice to the other chthonic gods (Hades' wife Persephone, for example, was also a goddess of plant fertility) and Hades might regard it as insulting if he was left out. Since it was clear to everyone in the ancient world that it was a very bad idea to upset Hades, he too received his share of sacrifice. The second reason for sacrificing to the dark god was more positive: through his name Pluton, 'the lord of many', Hades came over time to be assimilated with another god with a very similar name. Plutus was the embodiment of wealth, and Pluton was rich in souls.

From here it became standard to associate the god of the underworld with things underground, including mineral wealth. Mining in the ancient world was a particularly fraught business, but the market for gold, silver and precious gems was

insatiable, so the desperate and greedy reckoned it was worth adding to the risks of mining the risk of attracting the attention of Hades, if only for a greater chance of striking it rich. In these circumstances sacrificing to Hades could only help, since the god was going to be aware of people digging through the upper reaches of his realm in any case.

The connection between underground wealth and the lord of the underworld provided a way for the Romans to bring their own theology into line with the Greek. The early Romans had a rather complex relationship with the gods of death and renewal, and their concept of the lord of the dead was something of a mishmash of Greek and Etruscan traditions mixed into their own native Latin beliefs.

The Etruscans were already a well-developed civilization before Rome was even founded, and the Romans had a great respect for Etruscan culture and religion. Consequently, much of Roman thinking about the divine was filtered through an Etruscan perspective, a lot of which originally came from Greece and the Middle East. Early Mediterranean cultures were deeply intermeshed.

The Etruscan influence on early Rome left the Romans with a deep reverence for wolves, with whom the Etruscan deity Calu was often associated. Calu was apparently the early Etruscan lord of the underworld, though he too was later assimilated into the Greek tradition. There was much of the character of Hades in the Roman god Saturn, but the Romans had already decided that Saturn was closer to the Greek proto-god Uranus. Therefore, the Romans came to transfer many of the other characteristics of Hades onto the 'Father God', or 'Dis Pater', another ancient Latin deity who was associated with mineral wealth, as Hades had come to be. From there arose a sort of composite god whom the Romans called Pluto after the Greek Plutus, and his wife Persephone became the Roman Proserpina.

The association between Pluto and the Dis Pater was apparent particularly in the Roman Secular Games, which were held on the Campus Martius in Rome in honour of Dis Pater and his 'wife', Proserpina. The distinguishing features of the Secular Games were: firstly, that several of the events took place at night, and, secondly, that the games were a literally once-in-a-lifetime experience, since they were scheduled to take place once every 110 years. By some accounts an underground altar to Dis Pater and Proserpina was unearthed for this occasion and then carefully reburied afterwards.

previous page
Joachim Patinir, *Charon Crossing the Styx*, 1520–24.
—
This painting combines Biblical themes with a landscape from Greek myth. The kingdom of Hades is here clearly identified with the Christian hell, complete with lurking demons, while angels stand on the bank of Paradise.

First-Generation Olympians

Since painting or carving Hades was likely to attract his attention, the ancients tried not to do this. When they had no option Hades/Pluto was depicted as a serious-looking individual with curly dark hair and a pale complexion. He is usually identified by his symbolic animals, three-headed Cerberus and the screech-owl. Asphodel and mint also make an appearance. More controversial is Hades' identifying weapon, the bident (like a trident, but with two points). This has been seen mainly in Etruscan and Roman art, and it is uncertain whether the bearer is actually Hades. Yet oddly enough this is the one identifying item that has been passed to Christianity's lord of the underworld, who often carries a bidental pitchfork.

As a god of buried minerals and the dead, Hades was generally presumed to be infertile as not much grows underground. This presented an issue for later myth-makers as archaic legend had already given Hades several children – including, by an alternative tradition, the Furies, whom he fathered with the nymph Minto (whom a jealous

Marble relief with Charon ferrying souls across the River Styx, part of a sarcophagus, Roman, 3rd century AD.

—

At this time inhumation had replaced cremation and scenes such as this provide a deeper insight into the cultural values of the period.

opposite

Tomb from Paestum with Charon, 4th century BC.

—

A woman boards the boat that will take her to the underworld, welcomed by a ferryman with an alarming smile. In the scene below, those she has left behind prepare offerings for her tomb.

Persephone then turned into the mint plant). Hades' unexpected fertility was usually explained away by the tale that Zeus had actually been the father while in the guise of Hades, a somewhat improbable stretch, since even mighty Zeus tended to deal with his eldest brother with great caution and at arm's length.

There are not many myths involving Hades, perhaps because making him the central figure in a tale might attract the god's attention towards the teller. The most famous story involves Hades' abduction and marriage of Persephone and this is as much the tale of Persephone's mother Demeter (see pp. 100–111).

Hades' other involvement with myth comes with the attempts of various heroes to enter his realm – or rather to leave it again, since, as one ancient writer grimly noted, getting into the underworld was easy, but Hades was very firm about unauthorized exits. Accounts of the underworld are somewhat confused and contradictory, since our only descriptions come from a handful of returning heroes who had a lot else on their minds at the time.

Generally, getting out of the clutches of Hades involved working on his one weak spot – his indulgence towards his wife Persephone. Persuade Persephone and she would work on Hades, which is the route Orpheus took when serenading the couple in his attempt to win his wife Eurydice back from the dead. (Eurydice got her exit granted on condition that Orpheus did not look back to check that she was following him to the world above. As soon as he got close to the land of the living, Orpheus did look back, only to discover that his wife had not quite exited the underworld and now never would.)

Persephone also fell victim to the smooth tongue of Sisyphus, the exceptionally nasty king of Corinth. When Sisyphus died and was taken to the underworld, he was chained to a rock for his crimes, in some accounts by Hades personally and in others by Thanatos. Sisyphus pointed out how easy it was for an outsider to break the chains and persuaded his captor to be chained up himself so that Sisyphus could demonstrate this. After checking that the chains were secure, Sisyphus made his escape by persuading Persephone that his consignment to the underworld had been an administrative error. It was only after the absence of Death caused several exceptionally casualty-free battles that an exasperated Ares went to check why people were not dying and Sisyphus' trickery was revealed.

Sisyphus was a serial escapee (he had escaped once before under false pretences), so Hades made a deal with the trickster. When Sisyphus had successfully rolled a massive rock to the

overleaf

Unknown artist,
Aeneas and the Sibyl, c. 1800.

—

This painting manages to combine rich colour with the idea of a dark gloomy kingdom of Hades. The Enlightenment brought ideas of the afterlife much more in keeping with classical tradition than the underworld as Hell imagined by many earlier artists.

First-Generation Olympians

opposite
Pinax with Persephone and Hades, Greek, 5th century BC.

–

This tablet from a sanctuary of Persephone in Locri, southern Italy, shows Hades seated beside his wife with his iconic bird, the rooster, beneath the joint throne.

top of a steep hill, he could leave the underworld and Hades would trouble him no more. Unfortunately for Sisyphus, the rock was enchanted so that it always rolled back down the hill just short of the summit, so for eternity Sisyphus remains toiling underground with his boulder.

Other heroes whom Hades encountered included the distinctly unheroic Theseus, fresh from having abducted a girl to be his wife. The girl was Helen of Troy, who was at most ten years old at the time. While Helen's outraged family were tearing up Athens in their search for the missing girl, Theseus proceeded to Hades in order to kidnap Persephone for his partner-in-crime, a man called Pirithous.

A grimly amused Hades pretended to be unaware of the reason why the villainous pair had come to his domain and invited them to dinner. Hades provided chairs that bonded to his guests as soon as they sat, and so Theseus and Pirithous were positioned at the doors of the underworld as a – literally petrifying – warning of the perils of trying to cheat Hades.

right
Tintoretto (Robusti Jacopo), *Orpheus Imploring Pluto,* **1541–42.**

–

This scene from a Venetian ceiling panel shows Orpheus begging Pluto to return his wife Eurydice to the land of the living. In the original myth Orpheus relied more on his musical powers than upon oratory.

Titian, *Sisyphus*, 1548–49.
—
The tricky Sisyphus was in the end outsmarted by Hades, who promised to allow him to return to the mortal world if he could only get a particular boulder to the top of a hill in the underworld. However, the rock was enchanted so that it always rolled from its victim's grasp just before he reached the summit.

Theseus had only just begun turning to stone when he was rescued by Heracles. Pirithous was not so lucky because Hades was not a forgiving sort when it came to Persephone. Heracles heeded Hades' warning and backed off, leaving Pirithous to his fate. After all, Heracles was not in the underworld on a rescue mission but to capture Cerberus for his final labour. (Hades permitted this on condition that his hound was returned undamaged afterwards.)

The kingdom of Hades has been variously described, but never as erroneously as by that geologist who labelled an early era of Earth as 'Hadean'. Conditions in that primeval era were certainly hellish, with the Earth consisting of molten and highly radio-active rock, frequently supplemented by new arrivals in the form of gigantic asteroids, but this is in total contrast to all ancient descriptions of the kingdom of Hades. This was a quiet, gloomy place in which nothing much ever happened at all.

While novel tortures were occasionally devised for outstanding criminals, such as Tantalus and Sisyphus, most truly wicked souls were excluded from the underworld by Hades' gatekeepers, who included Minos, step-father of the Minotaur. It has been said that 'hell is other people' but in the underworld Hades allowed his subjects the equally severe torture of unlimited leisure to reflect upon their past lives, missed opportunities and failures, moral and otherwise.

When a soul had learned everything possible from past mistakes, the urge came to drift across the underworld and there, on the far side, drink the waters of the River Lethe and forget all that had gone before. Thereafter Hades allowed souls to depart his jurisdiction to be reborn in the world above, knowing that in due course he would be seeing them again.

POSEIDON
××
NEPTUNE

Great God, Master of the Seas, Poseidon of the golden trident,
earth-shaker amid the turbulent waves.

Aelian, *Animalia*, 12.45

As their contact with the Hellenistic world strengthened, the
Romans of the early Republic realized that they had a gap in
their divine pantheon. Their sky-god Jupiter could be matched
closely with the Greek Zeus, and – with a lot of fudging around
the edges – Juno could be reimagined as a Roman Hera. But the
Romans simply had no equivalent of Poseidon, god of the sea.

This was not particularly surprising, as we know from
archaeological evidence that the Latins were a hill people,
who moved from the Apennines towards the west coast of Italy
during the tenth and ninth centuries BC. Those living in central
mountain ranges have very little need for a sea god, and in
the succeeding centuries Rome was far from being a maritime
power. This began to change during the fourth century BC
and Roman mariners taking to the open sea found themselves
unsure whom they should beseech for safe passage.

In the end the Romans resolved the issue by promoting a once
relatively minor deity to the status of Olympian god and elder
brother of mighty Zeus himself. The chosen god was Neptune,
god of fountains, wells and rivers. In his original role Neptune
was of considerable interest to the agricultural, hill-dwelling
Latins, for wells and rivers play an important part in keeping

Nicola Salvi, Trevi fountain,
Rome, 18th century.
–
Here the god is shown at
the Trevi fountain in Rome,
appropriately enough as this
fountain is at the junction of
three roads (*tre vi*) that mark
the terminus of the Aqua Virgo,
an aqueduct that has been
delivering fresh water to Rome
for over 2,000 years.

First-Generation Olympians

crops and animals watered. We see traces of this in the Roman
tradition, where Neptune's major festival, the Neptunalia, took
place in the driest months of the summer – just the time when
one really wants springs and wells to keep supplying water.

It is highly possible that the Latins shared this original
manifestation of Neptune with the Celts, for the water deity
Nechtan has a remarkably similar name. Both derive from
the Indo-European root 'neb/p' meaning 'moist' (clouds are
neb-ulous).

We know little else of Neptune and his origins, because once
the Romans had found a god whom they could match with
Poseidon, they enthusiastically handed him his three-pronged
spear and allowed their new god of the sea to become Poseidon
in all but name.

Walter Crane,
Neptune's Horses, 1892.
–
Neptune became a horse
god through association with
Poseidon, who probably held
that role before he became
god of the sea. This painting
evocatively merges the two
aspects of the god.

First-Generation Olympians

While Neptune was something of a misfit in the Roman pantheon, Poseidon was very much integrated into Greek life from the very beginning. Indeed, so ancient a god is he that the origins of his name are unknown and may well be Pelasgian, an ancient language supplanted across much of Europe by Indo-European. Certainly, as soon as the Greeks learned to write, Poseidon was among the topics they wrote about. And while Neptune was promoted to the status of the elder brother of Zeus, for Poseidon this may have been a step down, for the earliest texts from Mycenaean Greece call him *Wa-an-ax* or 'king/chief'.

Even in Homer's *Iliad*, we see that Poseidon is remarkably hostile when dealing with his little brother. When ordered by Zeus to stop helping the Greeks against the Trojans, Poseidon tells Iris, Zeus' messenger, that he is prepared to back down, but only so far. Should Zeus stand in the way of his ultimate objective – the destruction of Troy – 'between us shall be wrath that nothing will appease'.

> *Strong as he may be, he is over-reaching if he attempts to restrain me against my wishes, I, who am equal in honour with himself... I do not in any way walk in the will of Zeus. Let him peacefully enjoy the heavens of which he is master, just as I am of the sea. However strong he may be I am not intimidated like some coward. Let him use his bluster to threaten his own sons and daughters, for they are obliged to obey him, as I am not.*
> *Iliad* 15,190ff

In myth, Zeus was the youngest of the three first Olympian brothers and he was probably the youngest historically as well – that is to say, the dating of ancient fragments of text shows that the worship of Zeus developed in Greece after Poseidon and Hades were already established deities. In one common variant of the Poseidon myth, the god, like Zeus, escaped being swallowed by his father, Cronus. Rhea, Poseidon's mother, pretended to have given birth to a horse, and gave one to Cronus to swallow while Poseidon escaped, hidden amid a flock of sheep.

Thereafter Poseidon had a very strong connection with both horses and bulls, so much so that Poseidon probably became god of the sea only after Zeus came to power – just as described earlier. Before the new god Zeus came to Greece, earlier references to Poseidon suggest that he was worshiped in the form of a bull or horse with little reference to the ocean. Poseidon may have become god of the sea for the reasons given in myth, except that the decisions were taken by worshipers rather than by the gods themselves. That is, devotees of Poseidon wanted their god to control a substantial portion of the cosmos and with the sky taken by Zeus, and the earth unavailable (it was shared by all), the sea was the next best thing.

Once he became an Olympian, Poseidon fought alongside the other gods in the war to overthrow the previous generation. To help him defeat the Titans led by Cronus, the craftsman tribe of the Cyclopes crafted for Poseidon his trident, a mighty weapon that could shake the earth to its foundations when stabbed into the ground. In the following war between the Olympians and the Giants, Poseidon's major contribution was to defeat one of the opposition's greatest warriors, a Giant

Mosaic with Neptune and Amphitrite, Herculaneum, Roman, 1st century AD.

—

This vividly coloured mosaic has been preserved through the centuries because it was buried by the eruption of Vesuvius in AD 79. It was one of several decorations in a small but richly decorated house in the doomed town of Herculaneum.

called Polybotes, and then chase him across the Aegean Sea. The fight ended when Poseidon threw the island of Cos at the Giant and crushed him beneath it.

Once peace had returned and the Olympians were firmly in charge, Poseidon established himself in a golden palace beneath the waves. Thereafter he sought a wife and settled upon the beautiful Nereid (sea-nymph) Amphitrite. She took some persuading, perhaps because Poseidon had a nasty temper, quickly aroused, as anyone caught by a sudden storm in the Mediterranean can testify. As with any male Greek god, Poseidon had not the vaguest concept of marital fidelity, although Amphitrite, following the Greek ideal of womanhood, was always chaste and modest.

A character altogether more interesting than Amphitrite is Neptune's wife, Salacia. She personified the open sea, and the Romans – according to the ancient etymologist Varro – added 'surging' to her attributes and linked this with eager sexuality, leading to the modern word 'salacious'. Perhaps wisely Salacia did not much fancy being married to the tempestuous Neptune and hid in the depths of the ocean, where she accordingly became the supervising deity. Such coyness made Neptune all the more keen and Salacia was eventually located by a searching dolphin. This dolphin became not only a star among Neptune's fishy retinue but a constellation of them. He can still be seen in the northern night sky just north-east of Aquarius as the constellation Delphinus. Less well-known and altogether more peaceable is another consort of Neptune: Venilia, beloved of sailors, who was the goddess of favourable winds and a following sea.

The god of the sea and his wife produced the merman Triton, who could raise the wind and waves with a blast of his conch-shell trumpet, and who acted as an envoy for his mighty father. Outside marriage Poseidon was even busier, fathering among (many) others the highly adaptable Proteus, Bellerophon, slayer of the Chimera, the hero Theseus, Rhode – after whom the island of Rhodes was named – and by some accounts the hunter Orion, whose belt is another feature of the night sky.

Among the most recognizable of Poseidon's offspring is Pegasus, the winged horse. If Poseidon had had a sense of shame, he might have felt it in this case. The god once saw a beautiful maiden in a temple of Athena and promptly raped her. Athena was outraged by this violation of her temple and

below
Attributed to the Theseus Painter, terracotta skyphos with Poseidon riding a sea horse, Greek, *c.*500 BC.

–

This two-handled drinking cup combines Poseidon's twin themes of the sea and horses, though in this case the animal's undulating body suggests a somewhat aquatic creature.

opposite
Attributed to an artist related to the Antimenes Painter, terracotta hydria with Heracles and Nereus, Greek, *c.*530–520 BC.

–

Heracles fights Nereus, the 'Old Man of the Sea', who was a relative of Poseidon and father of the sea-nymphs, the Nereids. At the time Heracles was trying to force information from Nereus that was vital to one of his labours.

First-Generation Olympians

Ignazio Danti, Poseidon rises
with his chariot from the sea,
detail of map of Liguria, 16th
century.

—

Neptune and his wife (preceded
by trumpet-blowing Triton, his
son and herald) dominate the
sea off the Ligurian coast on this
map commissioned by Pope
Gregory XIII.

compounded the crime by punishing the victim, turning her into the hideous Medusa. When Medusa fled to the wilderness at the edge of the known world, Athena allowed the 'hero' Perseus to follow and behead her. From the severed neck of the unfortunate Medusa sprang Pegasus, who had been conceived in the original rape and imprisoned in his mother's body by her hideous transformation.

Another of Poseidon's victims was a young lady called Caenis, to whom Poseidon granted one favour after the assault. Caenis asked to be made an invincible male so that she need never suffer that same trauma again, and he went on to become a much-feared warrior.

Poseidon was also responsible for one of the most feared monsters of myth, the Minotaur, though he did not father the creature directly. Poseidon gave a bull to King Minos to be

Spiotorno   I. di Albenga

C delle niele
S. Antonio

Imperiale

Lenguiglia

Araffi

C S. Eremo

ALBENGA

Cerno
Diano   Briano

Petra
Macare
Artelle

Finale   Loano
Calale   V. noua
Andera

Caftello
S. Pietro

Vorzo
Surua

Christophorus Columbus Ligur.
Novi Orbis Repertor.

Monaco →
R.Bruna

Mentone

Turbia

Castella

Bendignea

S.Agne

enzo
Anna
Spedaletto
Serboga
Caporaso
Gorbio

Riuaira
Beadi Tabia
Tabia
S.Audan

Bosena
Poggio
Valbona

Castellano
Peranando
Castiglione

Popiana
Busana
Doleaigna

Dolece
C.Franco
Sospello
Ribera

Vezzano
Virga
Rocchetta

Thetis rides Triton to deliver the shield of Achilles, Roman, 2nd century AD.

—

Thetis was chief among the Nereids in Poseidon's entourage. She was a daughter of Nereus and a descendant of the primordial entity Oceanus. This relief shows Thetis preparing to rearm her son after his armour was lost in battle.

returned to him as a sacrificial offering. Yet so splendid was the animal that Minos could not bear to kill it (Heracles did the job eventually). To get his revenge, Poseidon inflicted the wife of Minos with an unnatural lust for the bull, and from that coupling the half-human, half-bull Minotaur was born.

Many of the myths involving Poseidon show him as brutal and rapacious, because those living in coastal communities knew full well that the sea could be so. In the story of Poseidon's rape of his sister Demeter, she was well aware of his predatory intentions, and disguised herself as a horse. Poseidon then changed himself into a stallion and assaulted her anyway. Demeter gave birth to Arion, the steed that drew the chariot of Heracles. Again, we note Poseidon's long-standing connection with horses.

While we may simply consider the rape of Demeter to be one of the many Greek myths that are carefully edited out of children's books on the topic, the story makes sense if we consider the gods in their true role as elemental forces. Demeter embodies the corn and earth-shaking Poseidon the sea, so we can imagine a cornfield that was swamped by a tsunami. The land might no longer produce grain but be used instead to raise horses. In short, by inserting personalities into the interplay of elemental forces, we can see how the Greeks attempted to make sense of an arbitrary and often brutal world by turning natural events into myth.

Myth and reality could certainly merge in this way, one example being from historical times. The historian Herodotus

Panel from a mosaic
pavement with Triton,
dolphin and fish, Ephesus,
Roman, c. 200 AD.
—
This mosaic from Asia Minor
shows Triton with the tail of
a Cetos ('sea-monster' – the
reason why whales are called
'Cetaceans'), while a dolphin
carries his father's trident.

reports that when the Greek town of Potidaea was attacked by the Persians the god Poseidon did indeed protect his people. By sending an unnaturally high tide the sea god drowned the Persian invaders who were attacking the place. This seems to have happened just as Herodotus recounted, for scientists from the University of Aachen have found evidence of the tsunami that did the deed and the timeline fits exactly.

It is significant that even in the rare instances when Poseidon is being helpful, he accomplishes this with death and destruction, for unlike the modern Christian god, Poseidon was to be feared more than loved. It is hard to discover anything beneficial about earthquakes, and the thing that worshipers of the 'earth-shaking' god most wanted from their deity was that he refrain from doing it. Likewise, it is no coincidence that some of Poseidon's grandest temples, such as those at Cape Sounion in Attica and Tainaron in the Peloponnese, were at places particularly dreaded by the sailors who had to navigate those waters. Poseidon was worshiped to be appeased, and if his rituals were performed with sufficient enthusiasm, the best one could hope for was that he might leave people alone.

Attributed to the White Saccos Painter, oinochoe with Pegasus, Greek, 330–320 BC.
–
The winged horse shown on this vase represents this most unusual offspring of the sea-god – a creature of the air born of the union of Medusa and Poseidon in a temple of Athena.

While it is not surprising that the locations where Poseidon was worshiped were either near the sea or subject to earthquakes, it is perhaps strange that the god of the sea was not more worshiped by the most maritime of the Greek nations, the Athenians. According to myth, Poseidon did attempt to become the patron god of Athens, for the Greeks believed that such patronage bestowed prestige upon the gods and the more cities of which a particular god was patron, the greater his or her status on Mount Olympus.

The early Greeks were in the somewhat bizarre position of giving their gods what amounted to job interviews. In the case of Athens, there were two candidates on the shortlist: Poseidon and Athena. To show what he could do, Poseidon smote a rock with his trident and a spring spurted out. However, unlike the Roman Neptune, the Greek Poseidon was god only of the sea, so the water of his spring was saltwater – useful for a decorative fountain perhaps, but of no practical value. Athena, on the other hand, gave the Athenians the olive tree, which ever after supplied the Greeks with food, oil and a tough durable wood.

When Athena was duly made patron deity, Poseidon demonstrated his displeasure by sending a flood to devastate the fields of Attica that were accessible, but thereafter he left the Athenians alone. The thankful Athenians responded by building a splendid temple to the god, the temple at Sounion, which can still be seen today. Poseidon also got a consolation prize, for just as Athens took its name from Athena, Poseidon gave his name to the Greek city of Poseidonia in southern Italy where the temple to the god was considered the finest west of Corinth. (Regrettably, while three splendid temples do remain today in Paestum – as the Romans later renamed Poseidonia – these survivors are to Hera rather than Poseidon.)

Corinth, a city located on an isthmus, between two seas, was another excellent prospect for Poseidon the potential patron, and here he did indeed get the job. The Isthmian Games, rated as one of the greatest festivals in ancient Greece after the Olympics, were held in his honour. Some myths attribute the founding of the games to Theseus, son of Poseidon, and they were held regularly for about a millennium thereafter, ceasing only when the Roman Empire became dogmatically anti-pagan. (The very Christian St Paul may have witnessed these games, for he makes several references to athletic events in his letter to the Corinthians.) Perhaps oddly for games celebrated in honour of a thoroughly misogynistic god, it seems there were several events in which women could compete.

DEMETER
⨯⨯
CERES

Sing with the mothers and maidens, 'Loudly hail Demeter of great bounty,
lady of the corn…' To us will come the great, far-ruling goddess,
bringing with her the seasons and the harvest to keep us for another year.

Greek Lyric 5. Scolia frag. 885

One never has to look hard to spot sexual discrimination among the ancient gods, whether this discrimination is ancient or modern. We note, for example, that there were six male and six female gods in the Olympic pantheon (Hades, Zeus, Poseidon, Mars, Hermes, Hephaestus and Hera, Hestia, Demeter, Aphrodite, Artemis, Athena) until Hestia, goddess of the hearth, was bumped from her spot by newcomer Dionysus, the god of wine.

Likewise, when the cosmos was divided among the victorious Olympians after the war with the Titans, Zeus, Poseidon and Hades each grabbed a sizeable portion with no one even considering that the female siblings were due their share. So things have continued into the modern era in which just one of the planets – Venus – is named after a goddess and that is only because this naming convention is so ancient. (The pre-Roman Babylonians named the planet after Nana, their equivalent of Aphrodite, and the Assyrians did likewise with Ishtar, so modern astronomers would have been hard-put to overturn five thousand years of tradition.) After Venus the nearest astronomy has come to recognizing that not all goddesses revolve as moons around their male counterparts is Ceres, the only dwarf planet of the inner solar system.

Fresco with Ceres, House of the Dioscuri, Pompeii, Roman, 1st century AD.
–
The goddess holds a basket of grain, and a torch – which became one of her identifying symbols after her search for her daughter Proserpina in the underworld.

Ceres was the Roman goddess of the grain, the lady whom many still worship with their morning bowl of cereal. She was a very ancient deity whom the Romans believed had been worshiped ever since she taught humans the basics of agriculture and weaned them from a nomadic hunter-gatherer lifestyle. Since Ceres had no mythology of her own, it was a relatively straightforward business to identify her with her Greek equivalent, Demeter, the goddess of the corn. According to a much later writer (Arnobius of Sicca, *Adversos Gentes*, bk 2), the Romans made the formal identification of Ceres with Demeter in 205 BC by importing priestesses of Demeter and giving them citizenship so that this aspect of the corn goddess could be properly understood by native Romans. The combining of Demeter with Ceres did, however, involve a certain amount of effort to disentangle Ceres from her previous family ties.

The original Ceres was part of a group known today as the Aventine Triad. The Palatine Triad of Jupiter, Juno and Minerva represented the ethos of aristocratic Rome, with their gods of order, matronly motherhood and wisdom. The Aventine Triad represented the popular values of freedom (the god Liber from whom we get liberty), food (Ceres) and fertility (Libera/Proserpina). Liber was the husband of Ceres. Sometimes called the 'free father', he was definitely a more easy-going character than Jupiter, as he also represented wine and sex and was generally depicted with an upstanding phallus.

Identifying Ceres with Demeter meant uncoupling her from Liber and making her a single mother whose daughter (Persephone/Proserpina) was still a fertility goddess. However, in the new theology Proserpina's father was now Jupiter/Zeus, which makes sense when we think of the organization of the gods as forces and concepts: agriculture + order = fertility.

Whatever her family relationships, the pragmatic Romans recognized that their entire civilization was based upon Ceres and her gifts, and they honoured her accordingly. There were many temples to Ceres dotted about Latium and Etruria (the Etruscans probably worshiped Ceres, as did the Oscans and Umbrians). These temples were already established, so the main issue was not of building temples to the new god Demeter but of maintaining structures so old that their frames were often of wood rather than stone.

The main festival of Ceres in Rome was the Cerealia, an event lasting between seven and ten days from mid- to late April. The festival was designed to draw the attention of the goddess to the

Raphael, *Ceres and Juno*, detail of fresco from The Loggia of Psyche, Villa Farnesina, Rome, 1517–18.

–

This painting is one of a series by the artist which depict the trials of the innocent Psyche at the hands of Venus. She appealed unsuccessfully for aid to both Juno (right) and Ceres (left).

newly sown wheat crop and the need for her divine protection of it until the harvest. At the festival things kicked off with chariot races in the Circus Maximus and in later years theatrical and musical events were also included. A dedicated chief priest of the goddess's rites, the *flamen Cerialis*, thereafter took the lead in invoking a series of minor gods who served Ceres, each supervising a separate aspect of grain cultivation from ploughing and sowing through harrowing, weeding, harvesting and distribution.

Master of the Cité des Dames, detail of a miniature of Ceres sowing corn, from *L'Épître Othéa*, c. 1410–14.

–

Detail from a medieval manuscript showing Ceres in contemporary dress and a field turned with a deep plough (not representative of Greco-Roman agricultural practices).

First-Generation Olympians

Votive relief with scene of sacrifice to Demeter, Greek, 4th century BC.

—

Worshipers both male and female prepare to sacrifice a small goat to the goddess, who stands on the right with her basket for grain and identifying torch. Her garments are those of an aristocratic Greek woman, and somewhat richer than those of the mortals in the image.

Like Ceres in Italy, Demeter had a long history in Greece, and like Poseidon she was probably well established there before her younger brother Zeus came along. While Zeus is first attested in early Iron Age Greece (around 750 BC), we find Mycenaean tablets of almost a thousand years earlier referring to 'Da-ma-te', who is almost certainly the same goddess as Demeter. (Note the '-mate' part, from a primitive word root meaning 'mother', as Demeter's maternal role is important, both as an earth-mother and as the parent of Persephone, goddess of the springtime.)

The story of Demeter and Persephone is one of the most ancient of the Greek myths. All societies have certain types of myths, with the oldest ones generally being cosmologies, which tell how the universe supposedly came into being, and aetiologies, which explain how things came to be the way they are. The story of Demeter is that of how the seasons came to be – which to the Greeks meant basically a hot, dry and infertile summer and a cool, wet and productive winter.

We begin when Hades, lord of the underworld, sought a wife. Such was the nature of his job that the ruler of the dead did not have the chance to meet many living women, and he had a low chance of successfully courting any he did meet. Moreover, as one of the great gods of the Greek pantheon, Hades could not marry any common girl. He required a wife who would reflect his own high station (using 'high' in a social rather than physical sense, that is). After searching through an extremely limited list of suitable candidates, Hades settled upon *Kore*, 'the maiden', as Persephone was known. He did what any Greek man at that time would do and talked to the girl's father, who happened to be Zeus.

While Zeus was happy enough to see his daughter paired off with another senior god, he knew that Demeter would strongly object. (So too would Persephone, though this was considered irrelevant.) Therefore Zeus and Hades agreed that the couple should be united by the fine archaic tradition of bride-stealing, and Demeter would have to accept the *fait accompli* when it was presented to her.

Thus it came to be that Persephone received a highly unpleasant surprise while she was out gathering flowers. (This is generally assumed to have been in Sicily, though several other locations have been claimed for the event.) Suddenly the earth erupted and Hades made a near-unprecedented appearance in the world above, splendid in a golden chariot drawn by dark horses. Before the startled Persephone had got past her shock, Hades had seized her and whipped her away to the Stygian depths of the underworld.

No one under the sun knew what had taken place, though Demeter heard her daughter's final scream and became distraught with worry. As it happened, Demeter had to attend a state dinner that evening, the host being Tantalus, an Anatolian king. All the gods were attending the dinner and Tantalus, for some incomprehensible reason, decided to serve his own son as the main course. The other gods recoiled with horror when their plates were presented, but a distracted Demeter ate her way through an entire shoulder before she noticed the problem. Tantalus was duly punished (with grapes and water always tantalizingly just out of reach) and the boy reconstructed, albeit with a prosthetic ivory shoulder. His name was Pelops, and he went on to give his name to the Peloponnese.

Meanwhile Demeter had gone off in search of her missing daughter. All the other senior gods were aware that Zeus was somehow involved and consequently they refused to give Demeter any help. In fact, Poseidon, seeing Demeter alone and vulnerable, callously decided that this was an ideal moment to rape his sister.

At this low point Demeter found an ally in the goddess Hecate. Hecate the witch-goddess was something of an outsider among the classical gods, but so ferocious a character that 'even mighty Zeus gives her due honour', as the poet Hesiod pointed out. It is because she helped Demeter search through day and night that Hecate is generally depicted as carrying two torches. It also occurred to Hecate that while no one under the sun had witnessed

Gian Lorenzo Bernini, *The Rape of Proserpina*, 1621–22.

–

This statue has been praised for the flowing plasticity that the sculptor has given the marble and the contrast between the lumbering Pluto and lithe Proserpina. Pluto wears a crown, although this is not found in ancient depictions of the god.

Pinturicchio,
The Rape of Proserpina,
detail of fresco on the ceiling
of the Piccolomini Library,
Siena Cathedral, 1502–3.
—
This painting for the library of
Cardinal Todeschini Piccolomini
(later Pope Pius III) shows one
of a series of scenes from
mythology reinterpreted as
allegory. Pluto's chariot is drawn
by serpents and the god himself
seems less concerned by his
victim than the reaction of her
companions.

the abduction, the sun probably had. It was a truism on Olympus that no one messes with Hecate, so it did not take long before she had extracted the full story from Helios, the sun god.

Though furious with her brothers, Demeter lacked the power to take matters up directly with either, but she was far from helpless. The unfortunate victims of her wrath were the suffering hunter-gatherers who at this time made up almost all of humanity. They became collateral damage because Demeter went on strike and throughout the course of her divine fury nothing grew upon the earth. While this did not greatly distress Hades, who now had the prospect of becoming lord of all humanity, it did distress the other gods, who had become accustomed to being pampered with human worship and sacrifices and now faced the prospect of becoming lords of a lifeless, barren wasteland.

Peer pressure was duly applied to Hades, who was forced to reluctantly surrender his bride. As soon as her daughter was returned to her, Demeter anxiously asked whether Persephone had eaten anything while in the underworld.

First-Generation Olympians

Innocently Persephone replied that Hades had slipped her a few pomegranate seeds just before her departure. These seeds had sealed Persephone's fate, for Hades knew – as apparently Persephone did not – that anyone who eats while in the underworld is doomed to remain there.

Eventually a compromise was reached. Persephone would remain as the daughter of Demeter, and as such the goddess of the springtime, but for one season every year she would descend to the underworld as the wife of Hades. During this time flowers would not blossom, the wild wheat would swell and dry on the stalk and the trees would not bear fruit. Then Persephone would return with the spring (which northern Europeans would consider the autumnal rains) and new plants would sprout from the rejuvenated soil.

Terracotta hydria with the abduction of Persephone, Greek, c. 340–330 BC.

–

The central scene shows Hades riding away on a horse-led chariot, taking Persephone to the underworld.

First-Generation Olympians

Relief showing (left to right)
Demeter, Triptolemus and
Persephone, from the Temple
of Demeter at Eleusis,
c. 440 BC.

—

Demeter is shown giving grain
to Triptolemus, son of the king
of Eleusis, symbolically granting
him agricultural knowledge.

Some believe that mother and child were reunited at Eleusis in Attica. Demeter searched for Persephone in the guise of an old woman, because in ancient Greece elderly ladies seemed able to go anywhere. Demeter received a particularly warm welcome from the king of Eleusis in Attica and as a reward she taught the king's son the art of agriculture. Thereafter that son travelled about Greece in a winged chariot loaned by Demeter, spreading news of her gift to the people. (The Scythian king Lyncus refused Demeter and was turned into the first lynx as a punishment.)

The king of Eleusis became the chief priest of Demeter, and from that point on the rites of Demeter were celebrated there, as they continued to be for the next millennium and a half. Exactly what happened during those rites is unknown, for participants were sworn to secrecy on pain of death. It is known that over time the mysteries evolved from their origins as a Mycenaean fertility ritual to the full-blown celebrations that took place in classical Greece. Unusually for ancient Greece, initiation into the mysteries was open to men, women and slaves, the only specification being that initiates should be free of blood guilt from murder or manslaughter.

The prohibition against blood guilt is an example of how Demeter's influence spread to other aspects of human society, which was unsurprising in a civilization to which agriculture was central. Thus we find Demeter also in a secondary role as a law-giver, and also she and Persephone were involved with pregnancy and childbirth as part of their overall portfolio involving fertility. As chthonic goddesses (of the underworld), Persephone and Hecate also make frequent appearances in curse tablets, Persephone less because of her own dread powers than because of her ability to persuade Hades to use his.

On vases Demeter is immediately recognizable when seated on her distinctive winged chariot, though a snake or a pig lurking nearby helps to confirm the identification. While a sheaf of grain is a dead giveaway, another of Demeter's iconic plants is the poppy, which often grew alongside the corn. Given that the Greeks were well aware of other uses for the poppy, it is also very possible that opium played a part in whatever happened during the mysterious rites at Eleusis.

THE NEXT GENERATION

Athena ⚔ Minerva

Artemis ⚔ Diana

Apollo

Hermes ⚔ Mercury

Ares ⚔ Mars

Dionysus ⚔ Bacchus

Hephaestus ⚔ Vulcan

ATHENA
⋈
MINERVA

I begin to sing of Pallas Athena, the glorious goddess,
bright-eyed, inventive, unbending of heart,
pure virgin, saviour of cities, courageous.
Wise Zeus himself bore her from his awful head,
arrayed in warlike arms of flashing gold,
and awe seized all the gods as they gazed.

To Athena, Homeric Hymn 28, 1–6

**Athena Promachos
('First in the battleline'),
Roman copy of a Greek
original, 1st century AD.**
—
This statue of Athena as a
warrior goddess is a Roman
copy (found in Herculaneum)
of a presumed 5th-century BC
Greek original. Athena wears
her impenetrable goatskin aegis
and a helmet decorated with a
griffin – a beast that symbolized
mental and physical strength.

Once the battle with the previous generation of Titans was over,
Zeus settled down to a degree of domestic harmony. Not all
the Titans had been foes; indeed Zeus and his siblings, being
descendants of Gaia and Uranus, were themselves Titans. One
Titan who had been on the side of the Olympians from the
beginning was Metis, the embodiment of applied thought (as
opposed to daydreaming). It was Metis who had come up with
the idea of feeding Cronus an emetic so that he would vomit up
his children, who were incidentally the cousins of Metis, herself
a second-generation deity, daughter of Oceanus. It was Metis
who became the first wife of Zeus, though another tradition
believed that Metis was simply the victim of sexual assault once
Zeus decided it was safe to harm his former ally.

By whichever version, Metis was treated extremely badly
by Zeus. The now-king of the gods was still somewhat scarred
by his own upbringing and well aware that there seemed to
be a developing family tradition in which the ruling god was
overthrown by his children. Since the Uranus solution of locking
the children in Tartarus did not work, and the Cronus method
of swallowing the children had proven a disaster, Zeus tried a
new technique. As soon as he discovered that Metis was pregnant

he swallowed both of them, mother and child. Since this was one of the earliest myths concerning Zeus, there are multiple versions of the story, including one where he tricked Metis into turning into a fly before he swallowed her, and another when the swallowing happened before Zeus even realized that his beloved was with child.

It is uncertain what became of Metis once she was consumed. By some accounts, as the personification of thought, she moved naturally enough to Zeus' brain and there found so convivial a home that she made no attempt to escape, being happy enough to become the more rational part of his mind. This was all very well, but it did nothing to stop the growth of her child, who grew to adulthood within the skull of her mighty father and in the process gave Zeus the mother of all headaches that he thoroughly deserved.

Eventually Zeus could no longer stand the pain and he called upon the craftsman god Hephaestus to put an end to it all. Hephaestus, the only second-generation Olympian not a child of Zeus, decided to take the term 'splitting headache' very literally and clove apart his step-father's head with a double-bladed axe. Out from Zeus' head stepped Athena, already fully grown and clad in armour. (Where the armour came from is a matter of some doubt.) It is this event that put Athena upon the state seal of modern California, which went directly to statehood without the intermediate stage of being a territory.

According to the philosopher Plato, Athena may have received her name from this event (*a theos nous* means 'from

Attributed to the C Painter, pyxis with the birth of Athena, Greek, *c.*570–560 BC.

—

A pyxis from the Archaic era in Greece shows Athena springing from the head of Zeus, who sits enthroned clasping a thunderbolt. Hephaestus stands nearby with other gods and goddesses, including Aphrodite with a wreath and Poseidon with a trident.

The Next Generation

Gustav Klimt, *Pallas Athene*, **1898.**

—

Klimt's Athena depicts a powerful woman in a determined martial stance (though the owl symbolizing wisdom is also present in the background). The grey-eyed goddess looks calm and controlled, her pale face contrasting with the dark background.

the mind of the god'). However, modern etymologists politely disagree with Plato and believe that the name Athena comes from the name of the city of Athens, rather than the other way round as the ancient Greeks believed.

This is because Athena is yet another of those gods whose worship seems to pre-date young Zeus. A goddess very similar to Athena was a standard feature of the Mycenaean and Cretan pantheons, where she seems to have evolved from an animal deity (perhaps related to the Egyptian goddess Neith) to a winged goddess, to a goddess with a fully human form whose iconic creature was an owl. She was a palace deity who dwelled on the fortress acropolises of pre-classical Greece and to whom the kings – and doubtless their subjects – prayed for wise leadership. Most of the early references to this goddess use the Indo-European *men/min* prefix which we use even today in words such as 'mental' and 'mind', and the use of 'Athena' for this goddess seems to have evolved from her role as the patron deity of Athens.

This is also interesting in the case of the Roman Minerva, whom the Romans associated with Athena for the very

Athena in the *Iliad*

In the scene below, which happens early in the *Iliad*,
Athena makes the perfect cool-headed counterpart to
Achilles, one of the angriest men in Greek mythology
(and Greek heroes were hardly known for controlling
their temper). As soon as he begins to draw his
sword, Athena descends from the heavens. She
dissuades a rageful Achilles from stabbing his superior,
Agamemnon, when they have a heated argument
over who gets ownership of Briseis, a young woman
captured during the war. Athena encourages the hot-
headed young warrior to think tactically and not act on
a violent whim. However, she does allow him to abuse
Agamemnon with an onslaught of insults instead.

William Spence,
*Achilles Restrained by
Athena from Rushing Upon
Agamemnon*, 1818.

–

This scene is taken from Book 1
of Homer's *Iliad*, the epic poem
focused on the Trojan War, the
great conflict in which almost all
of the Greek gods interfered.
From left: Athena, Achilles,
Nestor, Agamemnon and
Briseis.

good reason that Minerva probably was Athena before the Greeks changed her name. That is, Minerva is apparently the Romanized form of the Etruscan goddess Menrva, whom the Etruscans adopted from Greece and who was already the goddess of applied wisdom and practical thought before she became Athena.

In many ways Athena/Minerva is the essence of what the classical gods were about. Despite their character failings, which were abundant, the gods were what stood between humanity and chaos. As the personification of rational thought, Athena/Minerva stands against the forces of unreason, blind passion and superstition: she is what makes us different from the beasts. No wonder the ancients ranked her so highly among their gods.

Greece in the Archaic era (approximately 850–550 BC) was a very rough place, and one area where strategic thinking was essential for survival was the battlefield, so it is unsurprising that both Athena and Minerva were battle gods. This did not make Athena a female Ares, and in fact the two were in some ways antithetical. Ares embodies the mad bloodlust of a warrior in combat and Athena the cool calculation of the general who sends him into battle in the first place. While for Ares an ideal battle ends with blood and guts all over the field, Athena's perfect battle culminates with an outmanoeuvred enemy being forced to surrender without a missile being thrown.

Reasonably enough, the Greeks much preferred Athena to Ares, and dubbed her Athena *Promachos*: the first in the battleline. Notwithstanding her strategic skills, Athena herself could throw a spear or punch as effectively as the next man – or god. Indeed, since Athena and Ares did not like one another very much the pair occasionally came to blows. During the Trojan War this ended with Ares running back to Zeus to complain that his unkind elder step-sister had beaten him up again.

You brought that senseless daughter into the world,
that murderous blight who lives for misdeeds.
You are mightier than any of us on Olympus
and every one of us gives you honour.
But that girl! Never once by word or deed do you
Stop her from doing whatever she wants.
No, you even encourage her, that creature of devastation
because you gave birth to her from your own head.
Ares to Zeus, *Iliad* 5, 872–880

By one account Athena played so rough that she took the name *Pallas* Athena in memory of a childhood friend whom she inadvertently killed during a friendly tussle. (They were jousting with spears, and Athena had expected Pallas to dodge. She didn't.) Another potential Pallas was a giant whom Athena killed in the great war between gods and giants. This Pallas had an incredibly tough skin, which Athena stripped from him and fashioned into the impenetrable aegis, which could withstand even the thunderbolts of Zeus. The aegis was usually portrayed as a sort of breastplate, rather than a shield, and has in the modern era given rise to numerous security and insurance companies of the same name.

Despite her prowess on the battlefield, Athena was essentially a goddess of the city – to the extent that this was one of her

opposite

Marble head of Minerva, Roman in the style of Archaic Greek, *c.* 27 BC–AD 68.

–

Statues of this type were common in Archaic Greece and are strongly linked with the influence of Egyptian statuary on Greek artists. Athena's faint, somewhat disconcerting smile is typical of these statues (*kouroi/ korai*), while her elevated status is shown by her headband and elaborate hairstyle.

left

Attributed to Meidias Painter, red-figure lekythos with the birth of Erichthonius, Greek, *c.* 420–410 BC.

–

At a time when Athens was locked in war with Sparta, patriotic themes were popular, such as this depiction on a lekythos (oil flask) showing the city's patron goddess assisting the city's legendary founder.

The Next Generation

names: Athena *Polias*. This was more pronounced with Minerva as the Romans tended to downplay her role in warfare relative to Mars. She was the goddess of wisdom who taught men the arts of civilization, from pottery to carpentry to the cultivation of fruit trees – especially the olive – and certain types of music. Athena allegedly developed the flute, but discarded it with a curse when she saw how it puffed out her cheeks when she played.

As Athena *Ergane* the goddess was the patron of craftsmen, a role in which she worked so closely with the craftsman god Hephaestus that the latter developed (unrequited) romantic aspirations towards her. It was as an indirect result

Miniature of Athena and Arachne at the loom, from Ovid's *Metamorphoses*, late 15th century.

—

This depiction of the most famous spinning contest in myth is from the manuscript of an anonymous French translation of Ovid's *Metamorphoses*. The eventual fate of Arachne is presaged by the large spider shown in the background.

The Next Generation

of this infatuation that one Erichthonius was born as a son of Hephaestus, and although Gaia rather than Athena was the mother, it was Athena who became the protector of the baby, who grew up to become one of the founding fathers of Athens.

Athena was also goddess of the art of weaving, a vital skill in a world where all cloth was handmade. As it happened, Athena had an early rival in the form of one Arachne, who was so skilled that she might have been able to best Athena herself in a weaving contest. The issue never came to judgment because for the contest Arachne produced a tapestry on the theme of gods behaving badly. Athena was so infuriated by a mortal putting on record the infidelities and injustice of her fellow gods that she drove Arachne to suicide. Afterwards, realizing that she had rather proven Arachne's point, Athena brought the master weaver to life again as the world's first spider.

This episode proves that, though goddess of reason she might be, Athena could be unreasonable at times. It was her vanity that caused her to side with the Greeks in the Trojan War, simply because the Trojan prince Paris had not awarded her the golden apple that would have acknowledged that she was 'the fairest' rather than her rivals Hera and Aphrodite. It was also pure vindictiveness that caused her to make a monster of Medusa for the 'crime' of being raped in a temple of Athena. Then once the newly snake-haired Medusa had fled to a distant corner of the world, Athena coached the hero Perseus to hunt her down and kill her.

While Perseus was generally a noble enough spirit, Athena seems to have had something of a soft spot for bad boys, and was advisor and protector of both Heracles and Odysseus – both characters with a somewhat erratic moral compass.

Athena also once struck blind an unfortunate prince who happened upon her bathing naked on Mount Helicon. Stumbling upon bathing goddesses was something of a hazard in the woodlands of mythological Greece, and upon reflection Athena realized she had been unreasonable and compensated her victim. Most goddesses were less gentle.

Other than Aphrodite, no other goddess has received the sustained attention of artists as has Athena. From vases and statues we get the image of a tall, somewhat austere young woman, usually helmeted, and from poetry the oddly personal detail that she had grey eyes. This was so distinguishing a feature that when the poet Archilochus complained that the Athenians had hung his captured shield in 'the temple of their grey-eyed goddess', everyone knew to whom he was referring.

The most famous temple to Athena is also the most famous Greek temple in the world, the Parthenon of Athens. This temple to the maiden goddess (*parthenos* means 'virgin') was situated upon the Athenian Acropolis, which like acropolises across the Greek world, served as the city's citadel of last resort. The temple's location there also reflects the role of Athena in pre-classical Greece when she was the divine advisor to Mycenaean kings in their hilltop fortresses.

In Rome Minerva's temple was on the Capitoline Hill, which not coincidentally was also Rome's citadel of last resort. There she was ensconced with Juno and Jupiter; the three gods were known collectively as the Capitoline Triad, the embodiment of the forces that had raised Rome to greatness. It is perhaps unfortunate that the greatest of Minerva's followers was the emperor Domitian, who reigned from AD 81 to 96. While Domitian made much of his connection with Minerva, either the goddess did not advise him or he did not heed her advice and the emperor's unpopular reign ended abruptly with his assassination.

Those wishing to see the almost complete surviving façade of a temple of Minerva should go to Assisi in Italy, where the front of her temple – apparently shared with Hercules (the Roman Heracles) – remains intact, though the building behind is now dedicated to the Virgin Mary as the church of *Santa Maria sopra Minerva*. This is appropriate, for in the Middle Ages when the temple was re-purposed Mary was given many of the attributes of Athena, including guiding her followers to victory in battle.

Baldassare Peruzzi, *Perseus slays Medusa*, from the Villa Farnesina, Rome, 1510–11.
–
This ceiling panel from a ceiling in the Villa Farnesina in Rome shows the end of Athena's feud with Medusa. The goddess's protégé prepares to decapitate Medusa, who is surrounded by her petrified victims, while the winged goddess Fama (Pheme in Greek) literally trumpets his achievement.

The Next Generation

Gorgons

Medusa was a gorgon by transformation – her two sisters, Stheno and Euryale, started out that way, and unlike Medusa they were immortal. Gorgons were often shown as protectors of buildings or of warriors (on shields), and baking ovens sometimes had a gorgon on them to prevent curious individuals opening the oven and collapsing the bread. Even Athena generally sported an image of a gorgon upon her aegis.

From top right, anticlockwise: Attributed to the Medallion Painter, bowl decorated with a gorgon's head, Greek, *c.* 625–600 BC; attributed to Ergotimos and Kleitias, terracotta stand with gorgon, Greek, *c.* 570 BC; terracotta gorgon plaque, Greek, 6th–5th century BC; and terracotta gorgon antefix, Greek, *c.* 540 BC.

ARTEMIS
⚔ DIANA

> In the streams of Amnisos, Artemis stands in her golden chariot
> and drives the speedy deer over the hills... attendant nymphs have
> gathered to follow her, and beasts whine and cower in homage,
> trembling at her passing.'

> Apollonius Rhodius, *Argonautica* 3. 879

**Fresco with Diana,
from the Villa Arianna,
Stabiae, 1st century** AD.

—

This fresco unearthed at
Stabiae, near Pompeii, shows
the Roman Diana with her iconic
bow. Artemis, Diana's Greek
counterpart, usually wore the
shorter, more practical dress
of a maiden.

The metaphorical opposite of rational, urban Athena can be found
in Artemis/Diana, the goddess of the forests and mountains, who
has a mystical connection to the moon. She is sometimes called
the goddess of the hunt and she certainly has a lot to do with
hunters, but this is because people in antiquity did not head out
into the wilderness for recreational purposes. Their main reason
for visiting the goddess's domain was to bring back meat for
the table and when doing this dangerous job they wanted the
goddess's help and approval. It should also be remembered that
the wilderness was ever present even in the most densely settled
areas of the ancient world – for example, hunters regularly sold
their catch in the markets of Rome. The wild and its associated
goddess touched the lives of all in antiquity.

Roman hunters sought the protection of Diana because the
problem with going into the forest to kill things was that once
there the hunter also became prey. Bears, wolves and wild boar
were particular hazards, though coming upon Diana herself
taking a bath was also a life-threatening experience, as will be
seen. Since there have been hunters for as long as there have
been humans, and hunting in prehistoric times was even more
dangerous, it is unsurprising that a goddess closely resembling

Mosaic floor from Villelaure
with Diana and Callisto
surrounded by hunt scenes,
Gallo-Roman, 3rd century AD.
—
This mosaic from a villa
in Gaul shows a variety of
hunting scenes. The centre
piece shows Diana with her
iconic hound and one of her
followers, the nymph Callisto
who was later turned into a bear
and afterwards became the
constellation Ursa Major.

Artemis had always been around. In fact, Diana was originally just 'the goddess' or 'the holy one' – that 'dia' part of her name is from the same root as '*dea*' – Latin for 'goddess'.

Because she had always been there, the Latins saw no need to give Diana a particular origin story, so when the Romans encountered the Greek Artemis, their Diana was something of a blank page onto which the story of Artemis could be transposed. Like Diana, Artemis was a goddess of the wilderness and while hunters earnestly sought her protection, she was also the guardian of the forests, the mountains and the animals that dwelt there, so much so that she was sometimes referred to by poets simply as 'the lady of the animals'.

In appearance, the goddess is usually shown as a serious-looking young woman with dark hair and eyes – unless she is depicted in her role as the mother-goddess of Asia Minor, which we will come to later. Given her role, the goddess could hardly be expected to traipse around forest and marsh in the long, flowing garments of a Greco-Roman matron, so instead she adopted the more sensible clothing of a maiden. This consisted of a simple dress reaching to the knees and, in the case of outdoorsy types such as the goddess, knee-high boots of soft leather.

Unlike Athena, who wears a helmet, Artemis is bare-headed, though she sometimes wears a filigree of flowers to symbolize her connection with nature. Since necessity demanded that Artemis dress as a maiden, theology had no problem with making her one and thus Artemis has joined the cohort of virgin goddesses which includes Athena and Hecate. This did not stop Artemis from having a number of boyfriends at different times, but it did lead to a complicated and often tragic love life.

As far as myth is concerned, the experiences of her mother gave Artemis plenty of reasons for deciding that virginity was the better option. Her father was Zeus and her mother was Leto, a Titan whom some sources call 'the honoured consort of Zeus'. It might be expected that such a designation did not sit too well with Hera, his wife. This anger became absolute fury when Hera discovered that Leto was pregnant and, in her usual charming way, Hera set about making life as difficult as possible for the mother-to-be.

First of all, Hera forbade any place on land or sea to give sanctuary to Leto, thus depriving her of anywhere that she could give birth. The Homeric hymn to Apollo (Hymn 3) gives a virtual travelogue of the eastern Mediterranean as it lists the places where Leto sought relief from her travails. To make things worse, Hera had Leto further persecuted by a gigantic snake called Python (the linguistic forefather of the *Pythonidae* family of snakes). She also bribed Eileithyia, a goddess of childbirth, to remain on Olympus so that she was unaware of Leto's desperate need of her.

Eventually Leto arrived at an island (given various names in antiquity) which floated unmoored to the seabed below. The idea of a floating island was probably derived from rocks of pumice which sometimes floated ashore after volcanic activity. From the perspective of legalistically minded mythologers, such an island was neither on land nor sea and therefore safely outside Hera's ban. Once a safe birthplace had been found for Leto's children, Iris, messenger of the gods, was sent to summon Eileithyia from Olympus to help with the birth of Artemis and her brother Apollo. (Hermes had other things to do, for all that Zeus – and only Zeus – sometimes used him as a messenger. Iris, the rainbow who links heaven and earth, was the more common message-bearer for the other gods.)

The floating island now took root upon the ocean floor and became Delos, sacred to the twin children of Leto. Artemis was a precocious child who, immediately after being born, assisted in the birth of her brother Apollo, and by this act became one of the goddesses linked with childbirth. Another side-effect is that because the birth took place on Mount Cynthius on Delos the names Cynthia and Delia became alternative names for the goddess, and like Diana, a popular girl's name with later generations. While still young Cynthia/Delia/Diana/Artemis obtained a golden bow from the craftsman race of the Cyclopes and was given her retinue of hounds by Pan, god of the forests.

Like nature, which she embodies, Artemis was neither fair not particularly forgiving, and when she and Apollo were grown they went on their own Aegean tour, mercilessly hunting down and killing all those who had refused to give aid to their pregnant mother. Naturally Hera, the instigator, escaped unscathed because she was one of the original great goddesses. When Artemis eventually stood up to her during the Trojan War, Hera was unimpressed:

> *You have the effrontery, you shameless bitch,*
> *To challenge me with your archery!*
> *Indeed, Zeus made you a lion against women,*
> *When he allows you to you kill off mothers in childbirth*
> *But now you contend against me – and it is going to hurt.*
> Iliad 21 470ff

Diana of Versailles, Roman copy of a Greek original (*c.*325 BC) attributed to Leochares, 1st or 2nd century AD.

–

This marble Roman copy of a Greek original (the goddess wears the chiton of a Spartan maiden) gained its name because it was given to King Henry II of France by the Pope and later installed in Versailles by Louis XIV.

The Next Generation

Thereafter Hera stripped Artemis of her quiver of arrows and whacked her about the ears with it until Artemis fled in tears.

Given the ungentle character of the twins, one might have expected that a woman called Niobe would have thought twice about insulting their mother. Then again, Niobe was the daughter of that Tantalus who fed his son Pelops to the gods in a spirit of scientific enquiry as to what would happen next, so evidently suicidal disrespect for the divine ran in the family. Niobe was queen of her native city and during a festival dedicated to Leto, Niobe asked why she should not be more honoured – Leto had but a single son and daughter while Niobe had seven of each and all were superior to the children of Leto.

Shortly afterwards Artemis and Apollo descended upon the city. Artemis killed Niobe's daughters while Apollo slew the sons until Niobe had only one child left – and no husband to father

Domenico Veneziano, *Diana and Actaeon*, **15th century.**

–

This painting shows Actaeon in mid-transformation while Diana and her attendant nymphs calmly look on.

The Next Generation

more, as Apollo had thought of that and killed him also. The grieving Niobe retreated to Mount Sipylus nearby and there was turned to stone, so that in the second century AD the writer Pausanias reported having seen a rock with a face rather like a woman's, from which moisture flowed like tears down the limestone surface.

Another who fell foul of Artemis was the hunter Actaeon. The most famous version of this story is given by the poet Ovid in his *Metamorphoses* 3.3, in which Actaeon came 'wandering through the woods, his footsteps directed by fate', until he blundered into a grove where Artemis and her attendant nymphs were bathing naked in a pool. The indignant Artemis splashed Actaeon with water, which transformed the hunter into a stag, and he was promptly torn to pieces by his own trained hunting pack.

Getting too close to the gods was dangerous, as Hippolytus, a favourite mortal of Artemis, discovered. Hippolytus took the male equivalent of his goddess's vow of chastity and so incurred the anger of Aphrodite, who decided to tempt him by making his step-mother fall passionately in lust with him. Hippolytus rejected her advances with disgust and with fatal consequences for all concerned. The step-mother hanged herself after leaving a note saying that Hippolytus had raped her, which led to the death of the accused. (For the full complex and tragic tale, see the play *Hippolytus* by the Greek playwright Euripides.) Deprived of her chaste boyfriend, a furious Artemis got her revenge by organizing the death in a hunting accident of Aphrodite's favourite human, Adonis.

Another who suffered for his relationship with Artemis was Orion, the mighty hunter. He became friends with Artemis and her mother Leto, and indeed he and Artemis became so friendly that Apollo worried that his sister was about to lose her virginity. Legends vary on what Apollo did next, but he either tricked Artemis into shooting her would-be lover with her own bow, or – as is more often told – had Orion killed by a scorpion. Thereafter the grieving Artemis placed Orion as a constellation among the stars, while the unrepentant Apollo did the same with the scorpion, which is now both the constellation and zodiacal sign of that name.

While definitely over-protective of his sister on that occasion, Apollo did once save Artemis when two allegedly invincible giants tried to rape her. Before the attackers could harm her, Apollo sent a magnificent – but illusory – deer bounding between the two giants. Each flung a spear, which passed straight through the creature and killed the giant on the other side.

Deer appear frequently in legends about Artemis. She herself would travel in a chariot drawn by golden-horned deer, and another of that flock (the Cerynitian hind, which was by some accounts also the nymph Taygete – transformed by Artemis to protect her from Zeus) was captured by Heracles for his third labour. This meant that the hero had to do some fast talking when he was confronted by an indignant Artemis while he had her pet slung over his shoulder. Heracles was allowed eventually to take the deer, on condition that he released it unharmed once the labour was complete.

Then there was Iphigenia, daughter of that Agamemnon who led the Greeks in the war against Troy. His leadership nearly came unstuck before it was properly started, for an unsuccessful hunt while the fleet had stopped off at Aulis caused Agamemnon to rashly curse Artemis – who responded by becalming his ships. After a long delay Artemis gave her terms for allowing the Greeks to go on their way once more – Agamemnon must sacrifice his daughter Iphigenia. This Agamemnon promptly set about doing (he was not a very likeable character), but at the

Peter Paul Rubens, *Death of Hippolytus*, c. 1611–13.

–

Hippolytus was a follower of Artemis whose dedication to chastity so offended Aphrodite that she set in motion a chain of events that led to the young man dying from a fall from his chariot (his name, prophetically enough, means 'destroyed by horses').

The Next Generation

last moment Artemis whipped Iphigenia away and replaced her on the altar with a deer.

Iphigenia became a priestess of Artemis in Asia Minor, fortunately with better terms of employment than the priest of Diana at her sacred shrine at Lake Nemi, Italy. That priest was always an escaped slave whose tenure at the sanctuary was terminated when another escaped slave successfully challenged and defeated the incumbent in mortal combat. How and why this custom developed is unknown, but the Romans were great respecters of tradition and they allowed this one to stand.

The status of the priest of Diana in Italy – an escaped slave – is indicative of the manner in which the fortunes of Diana and Artemis slowly diverged during the classical era. As Italy became more populous, Diana also became the goddess of the 'tame countryside' – the manor farms and suburban villas of the wealthy. Diana's role as goddess of the wild diminished and her role as goddess of the moon became more important. At the same time Diana became conflated with the goddess of the crossroads – Trivia (literally 'three ways' because a Roman crossroads was what we would call a T-junction) – while the Greeks usually considered this goddess to be Hecate. Thus, as Romans became more detached from the wilderness, Diana became more distant and her role more ambiguous.

Domenichino,
The Sacrifice of Iphigenia,
fresco from Palazzo
Giustiniani Odescalchi,
*c.*1609.

–

After demanding that
Agamemnon sacrifice his
daughter Iphigenia, Artemis
(top centre) saved her at the
last moment, switching her
with a deer.

In Asia Minor priests of Artemis were high-ranking aristocrats, for Artemis in the east took a different path and became the mother-goddess and protector of the entire region. Her temple at Ephesus (in present-day Turkey) had long been one of the Seven Wonders of the Ancient World, and festivals celebrating the goddess were among some of the grandest in the year. (Athens alone had at least three separate festivals honouring Artemis – one for her birthday, one celebrating the 'deer-slayer' and one where she was celebrated in conjunction with Hecate.) The Spartans would sacrifice to Artemis before starting a military campaign.

Artemis the virgin mother-goddess is one of those paradoxes found also in other religions, and in Asia Minor this probably came about through conflation with the goddess Cybele. Depictions of the goddess in this role are markedly different from Artemis the virgin huntress. Instead of a young woman with a bow, we have a matronly upright figure with a number of bulbous objects strung across her chest. These have been variously interpreted, including as bulls' testes as a fertility symbol or as simply a necklace with multiple strands of very large beads. Her worshipers were particularly fervent – and St Paul recounts that they treated him roughly when he came to spread Christianity in the region.

Artemis of Ephesus, Roman, 1st century AD.

—

This famous statue from the sanctuary of Artemis in Ephesus is a later Classical copy of an Archaic original. The statue retains a degree of Archaic-era stiffness and has clear influences of Mesopotamian elements. The significance of the bulbous objects on her chest is controversial.

APOLLO

None is so blessed with skill as Apollo. He is patron of the archer
and the minstrel; for Apollo is master of archery and song alike.
His are the tools of the fortune-teller and the prophecies of the seers;
and it is Apollo who shows doctors how to defy death.

Callimachus, *Hymn 2, Apollo*

If Artemis was the goddess of the wilderness, her twin
brother Apollo was the god of civilization. He embodied all
those characteristics that a cultured Greek or Roman might
appreciate – he was the god of music, beauty, poetry and light.
However, the Greeks and Romans did not associate beauty
with goodness and they well understood that 'civilized' folk
could be far more destructive and cruel than 'savages'. While
modern etymologists argue about where the name of this most
civilized of gods comes from, the Greeks had no doubt – he was
Apollyon – 'the Destroyer'.

To understand Apollo, we must meet the satyr Marsyas.
Marsyas was one of the early players of the flute – the same
flute that Athena had invented and then discarded because it
made her look silly when her cheeks puffed out. When Athena
discarded the flute with a curse, that curse retained its potency.
Eventually, for all the beauty of its music, that curse was to prove
the death of Marsyas.

While Marsyas played the flute, Apollo's chosen instrument
was the lyre, and eventually the question arose as to whether
Apollo or Marsyas produced the better music. A contest was
proposed, with the Muses as judges – which meant that from

Neoclassical copy of the
Apollo Belvedere,
19th century.
–
This version of the famous
statue of Apollo faithfully copies
many details of the original from
the second century AD, including
the cylinder in his left hand
(which was originally a bow).
The snake climbing the stump
beside Apollo symbolizes
wisdom and renewal.

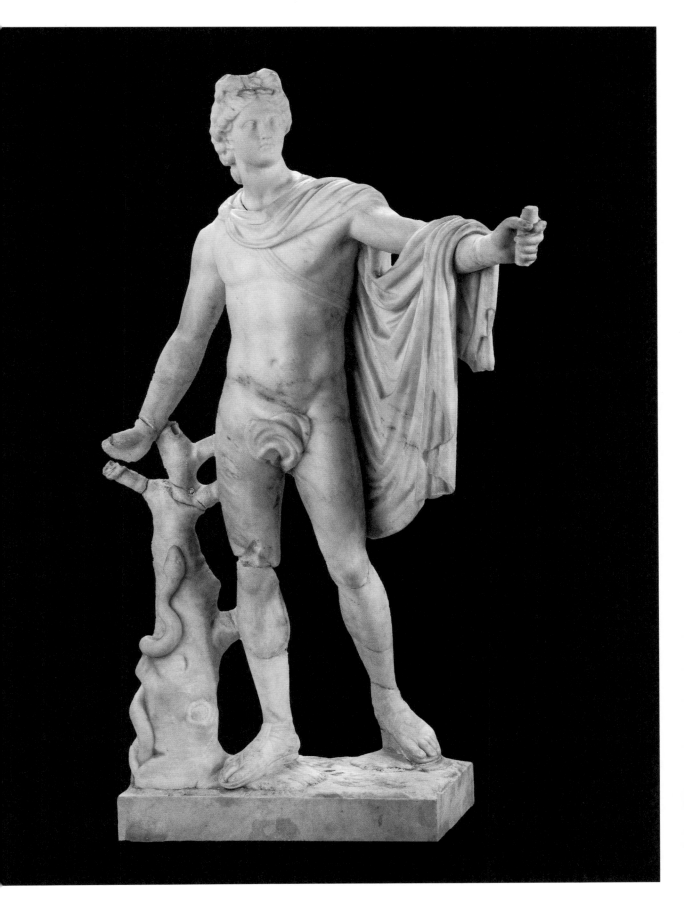

the start the event was rigged against Marsyas because Apollo was the accepted leader and patron of the Muses. Nevertheless, Marsyas played so well that the Muses could not help but dance wildly to his tunes, while the beautiful notes from Apollo's lyre moved them to tears.

With the contest adjudged a draw, Apollo did what civilized folk generally do when they fail to prevail against savages – he changed the rules and cheated. First, he said that the next round should be music and singing, and when Marsyas objected that this could not be done by a flautist, Apollo played his harp upside down and challenged Marsyas to do the same. When the satyr could not, he was ruled to have lost the competition – so Apollo skinned him alive. According to the Roman poet Ovid, the skinned pelt could still be seen in his time, hanging from a tree at the headwaters of the River Marsyas, a river originally formed by the tears of the musical satyr's fans.

In myth, satyrs were irrational creatures with poor impulse control. They were controlled by their lusts and emotions and lived for wine and sex. In short, they embodied the anarchic values that were the antithesis of the controlled rationality of Apollo – Marsyas was rock'n'roll to his classical concerto. The Greeks and Romans were very much in favour of Apollonian

Domenichino and assistants, *The Flaying of Marsyas*, 1616–18.

—

This fresco once stood in a pavilion belonging to a relative of Pope Clement VIII. The various scenes in the pavilion showed the superiority of the intellect over instinct and unreason – the very quality of the Greek gods most emphatically embodied in Apollo.

values and the violence with which Apollo punished Marsyas reflects the vehemence with which Greek and Roman culture rejected what the satyr represented.

It would be fair to say that Apollo was somewhat sensitive about competition when it came to his musical abilities. He took part in another contest, this time against the god Pan, who was rather good with the type of flute that still bears his name: the 'Pan pipes'. A panel of judges (who doubtless knew what was good for them) hastily awarded Apollo the victory the moment he first struck the strings of his lyre. The only objector was King Midas – he of the golden touch – who objected that the judges should at least hear Apollo play before they reached a decision. Apollo promptly gave Midas the ears of a donkey on the basis that these were more suitable for someone so lacking in musical appreciation.

While these musical episodes show Apollo's vindictiveness, there was an even darker side to this most ancient of gods. Apollo was a god of cities (the word 'civilized' comes from the word *civis*, which is Latin for 'city/town') and in antiquity city-dwellers were the principal victims of plague. It is probable that people were trying to propitiate the god of plague before there were even Greeks to worship Apollo. The early Babylonians sacrificed to such a god, and it is hard to avoid linking Apollo with Aplu, the god of plagues whom the early Hurrians and Hittites feared – a link made all the stronger as it seems very probable that the worship of Apollo came to Greece from Asia Minor.

Certainly by the time of Homer Apollo is the god of plague, his terrible arrows devastating the Greek host as they laid siege to Troy. Even in the historical record, Apollo is said to have assured the Spartans that he would fight for them in the Peloponnesian War, which started in 431 BC – a war that started with a plague that killed up to thirty percent of the Athenian population.

Yet a god who can inflict plague can also take it away, and the earnest entreaties of his victims that he do so gradually gave Apollo another aspect – that of a god of healing. With sickness as major a part of life as it was in antiquity, and Apollo's portfolio already crowded enough, eventually the role of god of healing and medicine was spun off as a separate person – Asclepius (the Roman Aesculapius), who was considered the son of Apollo.

As an interesting aside, the mother of Asclepius was Coronis, whom Apollo placed in the heavens as a crown-shaped constellation upon her death. (He killed her for being unfaithful.) Thus, by a quirk of etymology, the woman who shares her name with 'coronavirus' was also the mother of medicine.

Apollo may have been the epitome of culture and the embodiment of the perfect physique but he was never particularly lucky in love. His most famous romantic obsession was Daphne, who had herself turned into a laurel bush to avoid Apollo's attentions – and was only partly successful in this as laurel became identified with Apollo, and the laurels presented to winners in competitions dedicated to him have come to represent those at the top of their game in any field, from Nobel laureates downward. Then there was Cassandra, whom Apollo punished for rejecting him by allowing her to foretell the future, but never be believed.

There was also Sinope, whom Apollo promised to give anything she asked for if she would agree to have sex with him. Sinope took the offer and asked to remain a virgin, which left Apollo so baffled that he just left. Cycnus and his mother tried to escape Apollo's attentions by a suicidal leap into a lake, but hit the water as swans instead. Hyacinth died in a freak discus accident so Apollo, his grieving lover, turned his drops of blood into flowers.

Meanwhile Cyparissus, another lover, accidentally killed a pet deer that Apollo had given him and was so distraught that he turned into the cypress, a tree ever after associated with mourning. If Apollo had a successful romance it was with King Admetus, whom Apollo had to serve for one year as punishment for his killing of Python. Instead of coming to a sticky end as did many of Apollo's paramours, Admetus outlived his allotted years, thanks to pressure applied upon the Fates by Apollo.

Apollo's temporary exile from Olympus and punishment in servitude had been ordered because he and his twin sister Artemis hunted down and punished all who had refused succour to their mother, Leto, when she was pregnant with them. Chief among Leto's tormentors was the giant snake later called Python, who was thus promoted to the top of Apollo's hit-list. Snakes in the ancient world were considered semi-supernatural creatures and Python was especially so, because he guarded the sacred Omphalus stone near Mount Parnassus, at the point that the Greeks reckoned marked the exact centre of the world.

This location granted the power of prophecy to those with minds trained to receive it, and the site was therefore sacrosanct. Yet when he heard that Python was sheltering in his sanctuary at this sacred spot Apollo ruthlessly barged in and slew Python right in front of his priestess. Regardless of whether the prophetic Python should have seen this coming, Apollo's actions were considered highly irregular – after

Piero del Pollaiuolo, *Apollo and Daphne*, c. 1470–80.

A scene from Apollo's unhappy love life: this is the moment at which Apollo seizes the unfortunate Daphne who, rather than succumb to the god's advances, has herself transformed into a laurel tree. However, her escape was not completely successful as laurel leaves have been associated with Apollo ever since. Many depictions of Apollo even show him wearing a laurel wreath.

Giovanni Antonio Pellegrini,
Apollo, 1718.
—
This example of Baroque art
was one of a series by Pellegrini
that decorated the Golden
Room in the Mauritshuis in The
Hague. They show night being
dispelled by Aurora, the dawn,
followed by this painting of
Apollo as the sun.

all, who should respect the rules on impiety more than the gods themselves?

To atone for his actions, Apollo was exiled from Olympus for a year and after his spell in servitude he was required to hold funeral games for his victim every four years thereafter. These 'Pythian' games rapidly became established as one of the premier athletic events of the Greek world, second only to the Olympics in prestige. Furthermore, while the Olympics were a purely athletic event, the Pythian games, as befitted an event dedicated to Apollo, included music, theatre and dance.

Apollo then took over as guardian of the pythonic oracle, thus adding the role of god of prophecy to his portfolio. He had to do something about the name of the place where the oracle was situated because people had started calling it after the corpse of the gigantic snake, which had been left to rot. Up to this point the snake had been nameless, but now it was called Python, from the Greek for 'rotting', and the sanctuary was called Pytho (a name that Homer also uses).

Apollo had once recruited some priests by leaping onto their ship in the form of a dolphin, and therefore one of his epithets was Apollo *Delphinus* ('dolphin Apollo') and for some reason this was the epithet that was chosen as the name for the location of the oracle. As a result, one of the highest points in landlocked central Greece was renamed from 'rot' to an aquatic mammal and the place has been Delphi ever since.

While he was in the vicinity, Apollo either adopted or sired a child in a mountain community on Mount Parnassus. This child was Orpheus, who became the greatest (mortal) lyre-player known to humanity. Partly to keep Orpheus company, the Muses made their home on Mount Parnassus, which has become the metaphorical home of poets of later generations (for example, both Byron and Keats laud Apollo and his mountain in verse).

An interesting feature of Apollo was that he had no Roman equivalent, and indeed the god personifies so many diverse aspects of the human experience that he has no real equivalent in any other pantheistic culture either. (It is probably also because he embodies no single quality that there is no day of the week or planet named after this god.) As a result, the Romans simply adopted Apollo in his entirety from the Greeks, and he is the only god who has the same name in both pantheons.

It seems that the Romans adopted Apollo in the early years of the Republic in 432 BC, when Rome was smitten with plague, and the city dedicated a temple to Apollo *Medicus* ('Apollo the doctor') – in the hope that he would do something about it. Two hundred years later worship of the god was expanded to include the Apollonian Games, which, rather appropriately for this particular deity, featured artistic and theatrical performances alongside bloody gladiator bouts.

Alexander Rothaug,
Apollo Sending the Plague,
c. 1920.

—

This painting illustrates a scene from a story told 2,800 years earlier when Apollo in the *Iliad* of Homer smote the Greeks outside Troy with plague to avenge an insult to one of his priests. (Poor understanding of the connection between camp latrines and disease meant that Apollo often visited ancient sieges.)

The Romans also built upon the theme of Apollo the healer and saw him as a doctor not just of the body but also of the body politic. Thus, while the smooth-talking deceiver-god Hermes might be considered a suitable god for politicians, for the Romans Apollo was the god of politics – the deity charged with the health of the civic organs of state and of the constitution itself.

As a truly Greco-Roman god Apollo exemplified how the Romans of the imperial period came to see themselves as the heirs to Greek culture and felt that they were building further on the foundation that the Greeks had laid in the arts and humanities. Thus, for example, it became common for aristocratic and wealthy Romans to build themselves small temples to Apollo where they could listen to top musical performers or watch plays in the original Greek (although the Roman love of extravagance meant that some of these 'small' shrines could seat upwards of 500 people). The theatres were called Odeons – a word from the same root as a poetic 'ode' – and this tradition continues today, although modern Odeons are less fond of culture than of paying customers.

Given these different attributes one can see why the most famous follower of Apollo was Rome's first emperor Augustus, for whom Apollo was in many ways a model. For a start, Apollo hunted down and killed all those who had persecuted or denied shelter to his mother, and in the same way Augustus ruthlessly pursued and executed those who had been involved in the assassination of his adoptive father, Julius Caesar. Secondly, Apollo was the god of art and culture and Augustus so conscientiously patronized poets, artists and musicians that his time is still called the 'golden age' of Latin literature. Finally, and probably most importantly, Augustus promoted himself as the restorer of peace, order and the Roman Republic, and to whom should such a person be more devoted than to Apollo, the god who personified civic order?

In the later years of the Roman Empire, when religion began to trend towards monotheism, Apollo grew in importance. As Apollo Phoebus he had always been the god of light, but in time he began to elbow Helios aside and become more directly considered as the god of the sun. Thus Apollo became the proto-form of the later divine *Sol Invictus* – the unconquered sun – worshiped so fervently by soldiers of the later Roman Empire that church fathers and Christian emperors both inveighed against the god and incorporated features of his worship into Christianity. It is probably no coincidence

Terracotta plaque from the Temple of Apollo on the Palatine, Roman.

–

Here we see a girl in Archaic Greek dress decorating the Baetylus (sacred stone) of Apollo. This sacred stone symbolized both the god and his sanctuary at Delphi, where the stone marked the exact centre of the universe. The lyre at the statue's base serves to provide further identification.

The Next Generation

that 25 December was originally the Roman Festival of the
unconquered sun, which began its annual renewal on that
date. (This came right after the more general festival of the
Saturnalia – Saturn was the god of renewal upon the remains
of the old, so his festival was an appropriate way to end the solar
year and begin anew.)

The remains of temples to Apollo can be found right across
the lands of the former Roman Empire, with a particular twist
in Gaul, where Apollo came to dominate the religious landscape
rather as his twin sister Artemis did in Asia Minor. In Gaul
Apollo absorbed into himself attributes of many former Gallic
gods and thus had rites and epithets unique to that province

John Singer Sargent,
*Apollo in His Chariot with
the Hours*, 1922–25.

–

The Horae (Hours) were
goddesses who guarded the
gates of Olympus. As well as
representing Justice, Peace
and Order, the Horae were
collectively in charge of natural
time – that is, the changing of
the seasons and the rising of the
constellations. As such they were
particularly important to farmers.

(for example, as a horse god he was Apollo Atepomarus, and
as master of hounds he was Cunomaglus).

As the personification of beauty, Apollo has for millennia
been the subject of earnest attempts by sculptors to depict the
perfect male body, rather as Venus and Helen of Troy have
captured the changing ideal of female beauty over the ages.
Depicted as a young man, slender yet muscular, clean shaven,
with (literally) chiselled features and eyes that appear to stare
into some unfathomable distance, Apollo is the one to whom
people refer when saying that someone has 'the body of a
Greek god'.

HERMES
⋈
MERCURY

And so the Slayer of Argus strapped on his supple sandals of immortal gold.
These would bear him, swift as the gusting wind, over the waves and the
boundless earth. And he took the wand with which he can awaken
men from slumber, or if he prefers, lull them into sleep.

Iliad 24: 340–344

These days many know Hermes in his Roman form of Mercury,
the herald and messenger of the gods. Yet even this is not
completely accurate, for Hermes/Mercury was not a divine
postman who carried messages for any god. Typically, gods
wanting to communicate with mortals either did it themselves
or asked Iris, the goddess whose rainbow stretches between
earth and the heavens.

Hermes did act as personal envoy for Zeus and he also
carried messages for the gods of the underworld, but this was
more a side-effect of one of his main functions, as will be seen.
Nevertheless, it is as a messenger that the god is best known
today, with modern telecoms adopting as their symbol the god
whose image also features on the badge of the British Royal
Signals Corps.

Hermes has many other forms and many different roles, but
one thing links them all – he is what is called a liminal god, and
his natural habitat is at the edge of things. As mortals transition
from one state to another, Hermes is there at the border.
When we have to choose between right and wrong, or we find
ourselves somewhere between success and failure, or life and
death, Hermes is there.

**The Farnese Hermes, Roman,
1st century AD.**
–
This famous statue gets its
name from the Villa Farnese
in Rome where it once stood.
Identifiable as Hermes by
the winged sandals and the
remnants of his staff in one
hand, this figure is a Roman
copy of a now lost original by
the Greek sculptor Praxiteles
from the 4th century BC.

above
**Jacopo Zucchi, *Mercury*,
c. 1572.**

–

Mercury is one of the most
recognizable gods, with his
winged helmet, winged sandals
and caduceus.

That Hermes is a leading citizen in the state of uncertainty
can perhaps be traced back to his earliest role as a fertility
god in agricultural communities in Asia Minor. In those days
the period between sowing and harvest was one of continual
tension – would the rains fall in a timely manner, the plants
remain free of disease and pests, or would invading armies
pillage the crops, bringing starvation the following spring?

From the fields of Anatolia Hermes transitioned smoothly
to the pantheon of classical Greece, and he remained the god
of gamblers – but now the gamblers he patronized did not
just bet their lives on a successful harvest, but also on business
ventures, trading ships, a lucrative burglary, or simply the roll
of the dice. When the harvest was in, or a bet definitively won
or lost, Hermes had completed his role. Yet he had others still
more important.

While the Greeks and Romans did not expect that they would
meet the great gods either in life or in the afterlife, Hermes was
the exception. At the moment of death, everyone was guaranteed
a meeting with Hermes *Psychopompus*, 'the guide of souls'. In
this greatest of transitions – from life to death – Hermes was
present in this world to meet the soul after it exited the body
and then guided the deceased to the banks of the River Styx to
enter the underworld. (For this reason, Roman arenas usually
had a member of staff dressed as Mercury at gladiator fights,

below

Attributed to the Tithonos Painter, terracotta lekythos with Hermes, Greek, c. 480–470 BC.

–

Here Hermes is depicted on an Attic lekythos (oil flask). He carries a herald's staff, and the round object on his shoulder is a petasos, a type of broad-brimmed Thessalian hat popular with travellers.

who would insert a hook into the corpses of the slain and drag them off for burial.)

Given this grim role, one might expect Hermes to be a serious god weighted down by the emotional stress of the deceased and the pressure of his duties. Yet the contrary is true – of all the gods, Hermes appears to take life least seriously. He is always youthful, always a trickster god, the god of thieves and con-men and – in a not altogether unrelated field of activity – the god of business and the market.

The father of this most mercurial of gods was Zeus, which makes Hermes the descendant of the original proto-gods Uranus (great-grandfather) and Cronus (grandfather). His mother was Maia, 'a daughter of the Titan Atlas who holds aloft the starry sky'. Maia's romantic relationship with Zeus consisted entirely of his nocturnal visits to her hidden cave while Hera, his sister-wife, was sleeping in their abandoned marriage bed. Perhaps these furtive visits affected Hermes' outlook on life even before he was born, for later Hermes always delighted in clandestine plots and lawless escapades.

Maia herself is an interesting character, not least because even today she symbolizes the beginning of spring. She is the most important of the seven sisters collectively called the Pleiades, who in pre-classical times ascended to the heavens to become a bright cluster of stars that still bear that name today. For the ancients, the rising of the Pleiades signalled the end of winter storms and that the Mediterranean was safe for sailing once more. Probably not by coincidence this rising was in the month of May, Maia's month, which is also the month in which the Romans celebrated the rites of Maia's son Hermes/Mercury. Mercury has also made it to the heavens as a planet, but he circles the sun, not Jupiter. This is because the ancients noted that no planet moves more swiftly, so it seemed right to name it after the speediest of gods.

To say that Hermes was a precocious child is to put it mildly. While many parents dread their infant escaping from his cot, Hermes managed this on the day after he was born. Exiting the cave, Hermes came across an unfortunate tortoise. This beast he emptied from its shell, which he covered with ox hide and strung with sheep gut to make the world's first lyre.

From there the itinerant infant musician moved on to the fields where a herd of cattle grazed. These cattle were unguarded because they belonged to the god Apollo. Apollo is the god of music and the arts, but he was also famously vindictive as the flayed Marsyas might testify. There was no point in putting a guard on the cattle of Apollo because no one would dare to steal them. Until Hermes did.

Hermes somehow persuaded the cattle to walk backwards into a cave, so when Apollo came to investigate, it appeared that his herd had wandered into the middle of a field and vanished. Some smart detective work revealed that the cattle had been stolen by an infant, and since there was only one infant in the universe capable of such a feat, it was not long before a furious Apollo was standing over the cradle of the baby Hermes and demanding the return of his cattle. Hermes protested that Apollo must be wrong, as he was merely a helpless babe in arms. However, unlike Hermes, Apollo had not been born yesterday, and the thieving baby was immediately hauled before his father Zeus and ordered to reveal the whereabouts of the missing herd.

Hermes did so, but while at the cave containing the cattle he picked up his newly crafted lyre and began to play. His music charmed the savage Apollo, who was captivated by the instrument. Before long Apollo, god of music, and Hermes,

opposite
Andrea Procaccini
Mercury and Argus, 1716.
–
This 18th-century painting shows the moment when a cherubic Mercury puts aside the flute that has lulled Argus to sleep and reaches for the sword concealed at his side.

left
Attributed to Girolamo da Santacroce, *The Young Mercury Stealing Cattle from the Herd of Apollo,* 1530–50.
–
Here the artist has added a mythological touch to what is essentially a landscape painting. The infant Mercury removes a calf while an oblivious shepherd plays the flute. The animal is dragged backwards to hide the direction in which it was taken.

god of businessmen, had struck a deal. Apollo got the lyre and Hermes got off scot free for stealing the cows. Thereafter Hermes and Apollo remained the best of friends – an exceptional relationship among the fractious gods of Olympus. The pair competed in a foot race at the very first Olympic Games where Hermes, the speediest of the gods, chose to come a diplomatic second.

Another of the great gods with whom Hermes was friendly – very friendly – was Aphrodite, who later bore Hermes a child after a brief but passionate affair. This child was beautiful in a way that combined the features of both Hermes and Aphrodite and he therefore bore the names of both: Hermaphroditus.

Hermes did other errands for Zeus apart from carrying messages. He could even be Zeus' hitman, and his most famous victim was the giant Argus *Panoptes* ('all-seeing Argus'), the archetypal watchman. While the average mortal has one eye on each side of his nose, Argus had a hundred eyes

distributed all over his body. According to the Roman poet Ovid (*Metamorphoses* 1.595), these eyes went to sleep in shifts, so there were several dozen on duty at all times.

This unceasing alertness became a matter of intense frustration for Zeus because he was intent on the seduction of the princess Io. Hera happened upon Zeus just as he was about to reach the climactic moment of a tryst with Io. By a quick conjuration, Zeus hid Io by transforming her into an innocuous white heifer. The suspicious Hera immediately took custody of the cow and assigned unsleeping Argus to watch over her.

Stealing Io away from the ultimate chaperone would require a master thief and Zeus knew exactly the man – or rather god – for the job. Hermes appeared in the meadow disguised as a wandering traveller and lulled Argus to sleep with the soft

Bartolomeo di Giovanni, *The Myth of Io*, c. 1490.

—

In this complex painting we see multiple scenes from the myth, beginning top left with Mercury coming to the rescue as ordered by Jupiter. Disguised as a shepherd, Mercury approaches Argus, sedates and slays him, after which Juno with her peacocks sends the three Furies to torment Io.

The Next Generation

music of another new instrument devised by his son – the Pan pipes. (Pan of the horned head and goat's legs was conceived through a liaison between Hermes and another nymph.) With a regrettable lack of compunction, Hermes promptly brained Argus with a large stone as soon as he closed the last of his eyes, thus giving new meaning to the phrase 'rocked to sleep'.

Io went on to endure further tribulations before ending her life in Egypt (where she gave birth to the great-great-great-grandfather of the wine god Dionysus) and subsequently Io became a moon of Jupiter. Hera took the hundred eyes of the slain Argus and transferred them to the tail feathers of her emblematic bird, the peacock, while Hermes reinforced his position as Zeus' trusted messenger and fixer.

Among the first tasks allocated to Hermes was to implement the cunning plan of Zeus to punish mankind for accepting the gift of fire which Prometheus had stolen from the gods. The instrument of vengeance was Pandora, the first woman. Athena taught the proto-woman weaving and needlework, and the craftsman god Hephaestus gave her an irresistible maidenly form, which Aphrodite coached Pandora to use to optimal effect. The task of Hermes was to teach woman to be crafty and deceitful, a liar bereft of ethics or shame. Or so says the irredeemably misogynistic poet Hesiod, whose works shaped many of the later Greek myths.

Hermes then brought the finished product to her husband Epimetheus and smooth-talked him into disregarding the warning of Prometheus to beware of gods bearing gifts. Along with Pandora came her infamous box (which was actually a jar), which she was later to open and thereby unleash a plague of woes upon mankind.

Aesop often included Hermes in his fables. A good example is one – probably written after an unsatisfactory transaction with a cobbler – in which Hermes was ordered by Zeus to create a distillation that put a touch of deceit into every craftsman. Having distributed his potion, Hermes had a great deal of the stuff remaining and just the cobbler to go. So Hermes gave the shoemaker the lot. 'Consequently', explains Aesop, 'many craftsmen are deceptive, but cobblers cannot be anything but incorrigible liars.'

Like many a god Hermes was deeply involved in the Trojan War, where he largely favoured the Greeks. Nevertheless, when Hector, the bravest of the Trojans, was slain it was Hermes who – on the orders of Zeus – saw King Priam safely to the Greek camp so that he might ransom his son's body.

For the Romans, Mercury was responsible for breaking up one of the great love affairs of myth. Having fled burning Troy, the hero Aeneas and his gallant band of refugees wandered the Mediterranean until the refugees happened upon the newly founded city of Carthage. There Aeneas met Dido, the Carthaginian queen, and they fell madly and deeply in love. It was the unhappy task of Mercury to split the happy couple. He did this by conveying a stern message from Jupiter reminding Aeneas that his destiny was not the enjoyment of conjugal bliss in North Africa but founding the Roman race in Italy. Dido did not take this development well, especially as Aeneas proved too gutless for a final goodbye and snuck off on his ship before daybreak.

Giovanni Battista Tiepolo, detail of Mercury from *The Course of the Sun Chariot*, from the ceiling of the Palazzo Clerici, Milan, after 1740.

–

This androgynous depiction of Mercury, identified by his winged helmet, is painted in the Rococo style.

With his winged helmet and sandals, Hermes/Mercury is among the most recognizable of gods, especially when he carries his distinctive staff, the caduceus. This staff marks Mercury's role as a herald, for it was said (by the mythographer Pseudo-Hyginus, *Astronomica* 2.7) that Hermes once came across two snakes fighting and placed his staff between them. Thus, once again Mercury stands between opposing forces, though through a strange combination of circumstances, this staff has now come to represent the medical profession in the USA. (The American Medical Corps in the First World War correctly used the symbol when it placed itself between opposing armies to tend to the wounded, and in North America the association of the caduceus with medicine has proven ineradicable ever since.)

By some accounts, Mercury has another more personal staff which he has managed to keep out of the doctors' hands. This is more of a wand, which Mercury uses to bring sleep or to dull the gaze of those whom he wants to deceive.

right
Mosaic with Hermes Mercurius Trismegistus, Siena Cathedral, 1480s.

—

A picture of Hermes on the floor of Siena Cathedral portrays him as the master of arcane wisdom being consulted by scholars from east and west. Bare-breasted sphinxes carry a Latin inscription announcing the superiority of the Christian god.

opposite left
Sebald Beham, *Mercury*, from *The Seven Planets with the Zodiacs*, c. 1539.

—

This engraving is from a series depicting the Roman gods and goddesses identified with planets, and the zodiac signs under their control. Mercury rules over Virgo (bottom left) and Gemini (bottom right).

opposite right
Hans Holbein the Younger, Printer's Device of Johannes Froben, c. 1523.

—

Holbein designed this printer's device featuring Mercury's caduceus for Froben's business in Basel. Hermes/Mercury has often been associated with knowledge.

Perhaps oddly, given his role as a messenger, one of Mercury's sacred animals is the tortoise (or perhaps not, given the state of the postal service). A hangover of his original role as an agricultural god makes Mercury the god of herds and flocks, and he is also often depicted with a ram.

Finally, the crocus flower is sacred to Mercury, due to a freak discus accident that caused him to accidentally crush the skull of his mortal friend Crocus, who was turned into the flower so that his memory might remain immortal.

Unlike many ancient gods Mercury did not pass away with the classical era. In fact, his reputation grew in medieval times. This is because in Hellenistic Egypt one aspect of Hermes was conflated with the Egyptian Thoth, god of wisdom. In later centuries this led to a series of 'Hermetic' texts allegedly inspired by Hermes *Trismegistus* ('Hermes the thrice-greatest'), which dealt with philosophy, astrology and magic. Hermes Trismegistus is best known to us today through alchemists devoted to his writings, who named the slippery silver metal after Mercury, and also a type of airtight flask that is 'hermetically' sealed.

ARES

⋈

MARS

... deadly Ares, the taker of spoils himself. He held a spear and
was urging on his henchmen. He was splattered with blood
as if had been slaying living foes, as he stood in his chariot.
Beside him stood [his sons] Fear and Panic, eager to plunge into the fray.

Ares as depicted on the Shield of Heracles, Hesiod l.190ff

War was a fact of life in the ancient world – to the extent that
peace was generally regarded as the temporary condition of no
wars rather than a desirable long-term state of affairs. Even social
life in Greek cities and in Rome was shaped by the assumption
that eligible males would be on campaign for at least part of each
year. Consequently, it was inevitable that both Greece and Rome
would have a god of war to supervise their soldiers, give them
strength in combat and provide the courage to remain in the
battleline. Yet their attitude towards their war god tells us much
about the cultural differences between Greeks and Romans.

By and large the Greeks despised Ares, who is considered
even by his father Zeus as 'the most hateful of the gods' and,
despite being a warrior god, Ares spends most of his time in
myths getting outwitted, outfought and beaten up, especially
by his more capable step-sister Athena. On the other hand,
the Roman god Mars received a great deal more respect, and
rightly so. As the father of Romulus and Remus, Mars could
be considered the divine parent of the Roman state, and the
Romans were a deeply patriarchal people.

Certainly, the Romans took Mars very seriously. Military
training took place on the Field of Mars (the Campus Martius)

**Ares Borghese, Roman, 1st
century BC–2nd century AD.**
–
This marble statue is a Roman
copy of a Greek original
(probably cast in bronze).
Here Ares is shown wearing
the helmet given to him by
Aphrodite and the cylinder
in his hand suggests that the
original was holding a spear.

Pietro Perugino, *The Chariot of Mars*, detail from fresco, Collegio del Cambio, Perugia, 1498–1500.

—

Mars is depicted in the dress of a Renaissance-era soldier, riding a chariot pulled by horses, with his eponymous planet shining in the background.

just outside the walls of early Rome, and elections were held at the same location (with the voters being mainly the same people as those who trained there on other days). While temples to Ares were few and far between, the emperor Augustus put the temple of Mars *Ultor* ('Mars the avenger') right in the middle of Rome, beside the Roman Forum. Though the conflation of Mars with Ares was inevitable, given the syncretism of Greek and Roman religion, the two remained to a large degree very different gods.

Almost every ancient society had a war god, so the difficult task of tracing a god's origins becomes even more tricky in the case of Ares. A quick rule of thumb suggests that Ares may have originated in Thrace, since the place where myth asserts that a god was 'born' is often where his or her worship first began. The myths specifically tell us that Ares was born in Thrace on the borders of the sea of Marmara. (The 'mar' here has nothing to do with Mars but refers to *marmaron*: the marble that was quarried extensively in the area.) While the Greeks generally did not think much of the Thracians, it was universally conceded that warriors of this nation could fight extremely well, so Thrace is a good point of origin for a battle god of whom the Greeks had a low opinion.

Nevertheless, Ares the battle god was quickly separated from other aspects of warfare. His devotees prayed to him for courage and discipline, but it was recognized that the more complex issues of warfare required someone of greater intellectual ability than that which Ares demonstrates in his canon of myths.

(For example, he was once tricked into a bronze urn by two giants, and remained in there for months, hammering and howling until Hermes was attracted by the cacophony and secured the god's release.) Thus in Greece the intellectual aspects of war became the province of Athena while Ares was left to the actual bloody business of combat.

The Orphic hymn to Ares (Hymn 65) clearly shows what the Greeks expected of him.

To Ares, the unconquered, fierce and untamed who finds pleasure in missiles and bloody wars. You who can shake the firmest walls from their foundations, the mighty, blood-splattered lord, the killer of men who rejoices in the terrifying chaos of battle, in war's dreadful and tumultuous roar. Your delight is in spears and swords, the mad fury of unrestrained combat, in human blood and ruin.

As this hymn implies, Ares was generally neutral in a battle. Unlike, say, Athena who guided her chosen favourites to victory,

Jean-Auguste-Dominique Ingres, *Mars*, 1864.

—

This painting in neoclassical style is one of the few by this artist on a mythological theme. It shows Mars as a young warrior with the Archaic Corinthian-style helmet of an early Greek hoplite pushed up on his head.

for Ares the battle was an end in itself. So long as the fighting was intense and gory with suitable demonstrations of martial virtue abounding, Ares did not really care who won.

The exception to the Greek dislike of Ares was, naturally enough, the warrior nation of Sparta, which was the sort of place that gave boys a pet puppy which they later had to sacrifice to Ares to toughen them up emotionally. The Spartans considered Ares 'their' god to the extent that one of his statues depicted the god in chains so that he could never leave the place. According to a surviving text fragment of the writer Apollodorus (frag. p. 1056) the Spartans might even have performed human sacrifice to Ares at some point in their history.

There was also a monument to Ares in Athens, though this was of a very different kind. The story goes that Ares had a daughter who was raped by an individual called Halirrhothius. The furious Ares promptly slew the rapist, whose name (meaning 'of the sea-foam') should have warned him that the criminal was a well-loved child of Poseidon. This killing created a certain degree of tension because Poseidon was one of the three most senior gods, and not a power to be taken lightly. On the other hand, Ares was himself a formidable character and, more importantly, a son of Zeus, who also took the killing of his offspring very seriously.

It was finally agreed that Ares would stand trial for murder in Athens and a jury of gods sat in judgment of the case. Ares was acquitted, and the hill where the trial took place became known as the Areopagus, 'the hill of Ares', which became the site where the Athenians prosecuted crimes of bloodletting such as murder (and also the burning of olive trees, which was considered at

The Ahenobarbus altar, Roman, 2nd century BC.

—

This famous bas-relief shows Roman soldiers reporting for the annual levy. This is one of the few contemporary Roman sculptures showing soldiers of the late Republic era in full armour, depicting legionaries, cavalrymen and an officer.

least as serious). This was a typically Athenian commemoration of Ares – a place where the violence of the god was resolved by cool arbitration in the city of Athena.

Mars, god of war in Rome, may have been partly created as a response to the Greek Ares. The early origins of the god Mars are confused, as is the case with Ares, but it seems possible that Mars was originally the consort of an even older Roman war goddess, called Bellona, whom the Romans may have adopted from the Sabine people with whom they merged during the early Republic. The proto-Mars appears to have been as much an agricultural god as a military deity, but once Roman religion became entangled with the Greek version, it became evident that Bellona, being formidably female (she carried a whip and rode a chariot into battle) was not a suitable equivalent for Ares. So by this argument Mars, the shy farmer, was stripped of his agricultural implements, given a sword and spear and thrust into the battleline.

Nevertheless, some aspects of Mars the farming god remained. Most of his rituals and festivals take place in the spring, during the month of March which bears his name, and we know one aspect of the god was Mars *Silvanus* – Mars, god of the woodlands. The Arval brotherhood, one of the oldest priesthoods in Rome, was an agricultural cult, but Mars features in one of their hymns – a hymn so archaic that even classical Romans had trouble understanding it. Mars appears to have been especially linked with the life-force of plants, the vitality that makes weeds ineradicable and drives tree roots through the thickest concrete foundations.

This irresistible driving force certainly seems to have been something that Mars passed on to Rome's armies, for once he

The many faces of Mars

Mars has been represented in many different ways, from the older, bearded Mars Ultor (Mars the Avenger) to the young muscular man modelled on the Greek Ares.

From left to right: statuette of Mars Ultor, Roman, 1st century AD; statuette of Mars-Cobannus, Gallo-Roman, AD 125–175; statue of Mars of Todi, Etruscan, end of 5th century BC; statue of Mars, Leptis Magna, 2nd century AD.

had become Rome's premier war god, Mars settled into his position better than Ares ever did in the equivalent role in Greece. Mars became one of the senior gods of Rome, arguably second only to Jupiter himself in the veneration he received from worshipers. He had his own priesthood in Rome, the *flamen Martialis*, and numerous temples and festivals. Indeed, until the date was moved back to January (to allow the Romans to begin earlier campaigns in Spain), March the first – the birthday of Mars – was the traditional start to the Roman new year.

The Romans played down the role of Mars the adulterer (in Greek myth Ares was easily caught and humiliated when he had an affair with Aphrodite, wife of the craftsman god

Fresco with Venus and Mars, from the House of Punished Love, Pompeii, 1st century AD.

–

This fresco shows a tanned Mars with the plumed helmet of a Samnite warrior standing behind Venus, who is dressed as an aristocratic lady. Cupid on the right holds a rhombus, symbolizing fertility and protection.

The Next Generation

Hephaestus), but nevertheless associated him closely with Venus, consolidating a link between love and war that has endured ever since. There is a uniquely Roman myth on this theme: Mars also once desired the virginal Minerva as a lover and pressed the goddess Perenna to help him. Perenna was an ageless goddess (from whom we get the word 'perennial') but her long life had weathered her somewhat. She promised Mars that Minerva had been swayed by her persuasion, but she actually rather fancied Mars for herself.

While Ares is generally depicted as a clean-shaven youth, Mars is (when not directly conflated with Ares) a more mature individual, usually with a curly beard and generally dignified demeanour. This dignity took something of a tumble in the bedchamber when Mars came to lift the veil of the goddess he had been seducing and discovered that the well-veiled female was actually Perenna herself. The occasion became the source of a number of dirty ditties sung on the festival of Perenna, though since this festival took place on the Ides of March, later events rather cast a shadow over the date.

Although Mars/Ares was not married to the goddess of love, the pair managed to produce a considerable number of children between them. Phobos and Deimos (Fear and Panic) are predictable offspring of the god of war, and indeed the two remain so closely associated with Mars that they have become the two moons orbiting that planet. Less well-known are two children who generally took after their mother rather than their warlike father. One was Anteros, the god of requited love. The other was Harmonia, who was, as her name implies, the goddess of harmony, the counterweight to her more notorious relative Eris, the goddess of discord. While harmony is generally considered conducive to peace, the military-minded Romans hearkened back to her association with Mars and made Harmonia also a sort of divine drill sergeant, giving her responsibility for the smooth coordination of units on the battlefield.

Of the mortal offspring of the war god, many were brutal, murderous oafs, who were dispatched by various heroes (mainly Heracles) to the general relief of mankind. Another child of Ares who fell victim to Heracles was the Amazon queen Hippolyte, who became collateral damage in that hero's quest to retrieve her girdle for one of his labours.

While Mars was more restrained in his amorous pursuits than Ares, two of his children dominate the landscape of Roman myth. These are, of course, Romulus and Remus, the twin boys born of Mars from the Vestal Virgin Rhea Silvia. (With the name 'silvia', there is also an interesting link with Mars in his original role as god of plants and trees.)

Given that Romulus and Remus were afterwards famously suckled by a she-wolf it is reasonable enough that the wolf was considered by the Romans as sacred to Mars, though another totemic animal of the god – the woodpecker – is more surprising. Animals sacrificed to Mars had to be male and not castrated (i.e. bulls, rather than oxen).

However, Mars was not universally revered in Rome. The Romans admired him for his contribution to Rome's glory

Sandro Botticelli,
*Venus and Mars, c.*1485.
–
The oblong shape of this painting suggests that it was originally embedded in an item of furniture, perhaps a headboard, as Mars sleeps so soundly that even a conch blown in his ear by a playful faun does not waken him. Venus is depicted as unusually demure and clothed.

The Next Generation

on foreign battlefields, yet recognized his malign influence on the civil strife that regularly tore apart the state. Seneca the Younger probably had this aspect of Rome's war god in mind when he wrote:

Warlike Mars invented new forms of strife and a thousand ways to die. From this source rivers of blood stained the nations and turned the sea red. Crime raged freely through every home and … brother killed brother while fathers perished at the hands of their sons.
Seneca, *Phaedra* 540

DIONYSUS
✕✕
BACCHUS

On Bacchae! Bacchae, move!
Bring home our noisy god, son of a god.
Bring great Dionysus from the mountains of Phrygia
To the wide roads of Greece.
All hail!

Chorus in *The Bacchae*, Euripides, 112–118

In the case of the god known to the Romans as Bacchus and to the Greeks as Dionysus, the myths associated with the god seem to be remarkably similar to what anthropology and archaeology can trace of his worship.

Archaeological discoveries have shown clearly that in Greece Dionysus was worshiped in the pre-classical era, and that there are strong connections with Egypt in this first manifestation of the god. His name, written in Linear B upon clay and pottery fragments dating from the time of Mycenaean Greece (around 1500 BC), shows that in his first incarnation Dionysus was another of those gods who pre-dated the Olympians, even though later Greek myth assumes him to be the youngest of the twelve.

In around 1230 BC came the mysterious collapse at the end of the Bronze Age – an unexplained cataclysm which destroyed many civilizations in the western Mediterranean, including those of Crete and Mycenaean Greece. A dark age followed in which the worship of Dionysus seems to have vanished from mainland Greece. Yet the wine god did not disappear from human consciousness altogether, for either his cult survived in eastern Anatolia and in the lands bordering India, or at the least a very similar god was worshiped there.

Michelangelo, *Bacchus*, 1496–97.

–

This statue shows Bacchus in heroic pose, but Michelangelo has shifted the centre of gravity to show the god as somewhat unsteady on his feet, reeling and with his eyes fixed on his goblet of wine.

The Next Generation

Gradually the worship of Dionysus spread to the west again, into what was now classical Greece. To say that this new version of Dionysus was not the usual kind of god is putting it mildly. In a society that prized rationality and self-control, the god Dionysus now embodied creative madness, irrational frenzy and drunken ecstasy (the latter word coming from the Greek meaning 'to be outside oneself').

In a culture that worked hard to repress female sexuality and self-expression, female followers of Dionysus (named Maenads or Bacchantes) danced wildly in revealing clothing, and (according to dark mutterings by opponents of the cult) threw

Mosaic with Dionysus riding a Leopard, House of Masks, Delos, c. 120–80 BC.
—
The leopard was one of the god's iconic animals and he is often shown riding a chariot pulled by these cats. This portrayal comes from the Greek island of Delos, which appears to have been used as a way-station by travelling actors.

The Next Generation

themselves into impassioned orgies involving sex with satyrs and any available menfolk, all while consuming prodigious quantities of wine. As a further demonstration of their uninhibited abandonment of contemporary standards, these worshipers might tear to pieces any animal they encountered and gorge upon the raw, and in some cases still living, flesh.

It is legitimate to ask how such a god came to be recognized by the somewhat strait-laced Greek states and the almost puritanical Roman Republic. Yet the answer might lie in the very strictness with which Greco-Roman culture repressed unorthodox behaviour. The Greeks and Romans were at their core highly pragmatic and realized that it was impossible to eliminate the human need to cut loose every once in a while. If people were going to go noisily berserk on occasion, it was best that they do so within a recognized social structure. In short, Dionysus was the officially sanctioned god of the counterculture.

Naturally enough, not every ruler accepted Dionysian revels as inevitable, but gradually the cult of Dionysus took root, first in classical Greece and then in Rome, where the legend of the twice-born god made it very easy for the Romans to repurpose their god Liber (see p. 102) as the first incarnation of the later god Bacchus.

When we turn from historical anthropology to Greco-Roman myth we find the same story, albeit rendered much more colourfully. Dionysus was the child of Zeus, who impregnated Persephone while she was the consort of Hades, transforming himself into a snake and wriggling into the underworld to do so. This nefarious deed (Persephone was, after all, Zeus' daughter and sister-in-law) led to the birth of Dionysus shortly before the war with the Giants, which almost toppled the gods from the heights of Mount Olympus.

Dionysus took part in the struggle but his youth and inexperience caused him to be trapped by several Giants who literally ripped him to pieces. After the battle, a grieving Zeus retrieved the scraps of the young god's heart, for which he had a plan. With the help of various magical concoctions, Zeus made these scraps into a brew which he fed to his current paramour, a Theban princess called Semele. (It probably came as a relief to the rest of womankind that Zeus seldom set his sights lower than princesses.) In due course, a reconstituted baby Dionysus began to grow in her womb.

Semele was aware that there were more exciting ways to get pregnant and she readily agreed when Hera pointed out that for truly epic sex Zeus should approach her 'as he approached his wife'. Semele tricked Zeus into doing just that and discovered that gods presented their human aspect to humans for a reason. In the presence of the true nature of Zeus, Semele was promptly blasted to atoms. Baby Dionysus was made of sterner stuff, being largely divine himself, and Zeus hastily made a cut in his thigh and sewed the baby within, thus turning himself into a sort of *ad hoc* incubator.

Yet the malice of Hera was not satisfied by the destruction of Semele. While it was harder to kill the divine Dionysus, once he was grown to manhood Hera succeeded in driving him mad. While deranged, Dionysus left Greece and wandered all the way to the borders of India. In his travels he picked up the panthers that henceforth pulled his chariot and struck up a lifelong friendship with the satyrs, a species who themselves knew a thing or two about being irrational.

As Dionysus wandered back westwards, a Phrygian king treated hospitably one of these satyrs who had become drunk enough to get separated from the Dionysian retinue. Dionysus offered this King Midas whatever he wanted as a reward and the unfortunate monarch asked that everything he touched would turn to gold. One aurified daughter and several inedible golden meals later, Midas realized he had wished upon himself a life-threatening affliction. Fortunately Dionysus was able to cure the king by having him bathe in a nearby river. The sands of this river immediately turned to gold – much to the delight of the king living downstream, whom the accumulated sand made as rich as, well, himself – Croesus.

At about this time Dionysus was cured of madness by Hera's mother Rhea, whom the locals worshiped as the goddess Cybele. Thus Dionysus returned to Greece, having survived death, rebirth, exile, madness and countless orgies with his satyr companions. Yet the young god was still very much finding his feet as a deity, as is shown by the story that he was once kidnapped by pirates while taking a ship across the Aegean. True, Dionysus promptly turned the miscreants into dolphins, but no other god ever needed to get about by booking passage on a ship.

It may have been while on his maritime adventures that Dionysus came across the distressed Ariadne, who had been abandoned by the heroic but morally deficient Theseus after she had helped him on his quest to slay the Minotaur. Dionysus was so entranced by the princess that he offered her the moon and the stars if she would marry him. In the end Ariadne only got the stars, since the crown she wore for her wedding was placed

top
Attributed to the Frignano Painter, skyphos with a dancing maenad, Greek, *c.*375–350 BC.

bottom left
Attributed to the Lycurgus Painter, situla with Dionysus among satyrs and maenads, Apulian, *c.*360–340 BC.

bottom right
Attributed to the Captives Group, stamnos with satyr and maenad, Faliscan, *c.*350 BC.

–

Dionysian revels were a popular theme on vessels and this selection shows: a maenad throwing her head back, carried away by the god's influence; Dionysus himself riding a chariot pulled by griffins, while a satyr serves wine to women below; and a maenad and satyr dancing together.

in the heavens to become the constellation Corona Borealis. However, as the namesake for the main launch rocket of the European space programme, Ariadne might yet also attain the moon.

In Greece Dionysus encountered considerable scepticism about his supposed divinity, nowhere more than in his native city of Thebes. The current king of Thebes was a man called Pentheus, who was understandably sceptical when his long-lost cousin (through the line of his mother Semele) returned claiming to be a god. Pentheus strictly forbade the worship of Dionysus in Thebes and was none too happy when he heard that the rites of Dionysus were nevertheless being celebrated on a nearby mountainside.

The king decided to spy on the ritual, doubtless in the hope of catching some female followers in mid-orgy. Rather to his surprise Pentheus discovered that his aunt and mother were among the Maenads, and to his even greater surprise they did not recognize him. Instead they took him for a lion and fiercely ripped him to pieces. (Those who follow the legends of Dionysus will be aware that violent dismemberment is something of an ongoing theme.) The full story of this incident has been rendered into deathless verse and can still be read today in Euripides' play *The Bacchae*.

In Thrace a similarly sceptical king resisted the worship of Dionysus even after he was deceived into cutting into bits what he believed was a stand of ivy sacred to the god. It turned out that Dionysus had deceived him and he had violently dismembered his own child. Since this somehow did not make

William-Adolphe Bouguereau, *Bacchante on a Panther*, 1855.

—

A female follower of Bacchus rides a leopard and holds a thyrsus, a staff usually topped by a pine cone (though vines or berries are also possible), which was carried by those indulging in Bacchic rites.

The Next Generation

Piero di Cosimo,
*The Discovery of Honey by
Bacchus, c.*1499.

–

A whimsical painting in which
Bacchus and Ariadne (right,
foreground) are surrounded
by satyrs and maenads, who
discover honey in a hollow
tree. This is a step towards
civilization, symbolized by the
town on the far left, which is
safe and idyllic, while nature
on the right is distinctly
threatening.

the king any more welcoming to Dionysus, the god inflicted
the land with a famine. (Though he specialized in vines and
especially grapes, Dionysus was basically a fertility god.) After
two bad seasons the people of Thrace decided that they had
suffered enough from their king's vendetta, and ripped the man
to pieces, having evidently noted that this was how Dionysus
liked things done.

Perhaps because they were protected by their patron goddess,
when they offended Dionysus the Athenians got off more lightly.
The Athenians already had a festival called the Dionysia in which
they celebrated the grape harvest, and at this festival they were
presented with a roughly carved statue of Dionysus from the
nearby town of Eleutherae. By this time the Athenians had highly
sophisticated tastes in sculpture and they rejected the crude
Eleutherean offering with contempt. This caused the annoyed
Dionysus to smite the Athenians with a plague, the exact nature
of which the Athenians were somewhat bashful about. It evidently
concerned male genitalia, for in parades celebrating Dionysus in
later eras, large phalluses were waved about by the populace in
gratitude that the menfolk now had these in working order.

The Athenians got out from under the hammer of Dionysus'
curse by instituting a festival of plays dedicated to the god. By
the classical era the Great Dionysia had become the premier

Fresco depicting (probably
Bacchic) initiation rites, from
the House of the Mysteries,
Pompeii, 1st century BC.
—
These panels are part of a
series believed to show a young
woman being inducted into a
mystery cult.

theatrical event in the ancient world. Plays still performed around the world today, such as the works of Aeschylus, Aristophanes and Euripides, were first seen at this festival, which attracted tourists from all over the Mediterranean.

While Dionysus and his worship became an accepted fact of life in Greece, the Republican Romans had a harder time adjusting to a god who embodied uninhibited drunkenness and freestyle sex. Theirs was a society where a husband could legitimately beat his wife to death if he smelled wine on her breath, and where once a senator lost his rank because he had kissed his wife in front of their daughter.

Yet into even this society Dionysus insinuated himself. This was partly because the Romans were expanding their state southward across Italy and absorbed Greek peoples in places such as Capua and Naples, where the worship of Dionysus was already established. In Rome itself, Bacchus was considered as the reborn form of the people's god Liber. In the mid-Republic (around 264–133 BC) Roman society was impressively upwardly mobile, and as a result the worship of Bacchus moved up from the lower to the middle classes and finally into the ranks of

Krater with Dionysus and dolphins, Greek, c. 540 BC.
—
This famous Greek drinking cup shows the legend of Dionysus being threatened by pirates while taking a ship to Greece. The god turned his would-be captors to dolphins who are shown here swimming around his ship while vines sprout in the background.

The Next Generation

the aristocracy, where the arrival of the wine god appalled the authorities.

The historian Livy gives an account of Bacchic revels in tones rather similar to the shock-horror hysteria of modern tabloids:

> *At night, aroused by wine, men mingled with women, young with old, with all sense of modesty extinguished, so that every imaginable form of obscenity took place... violence was concealed because the voices of those crying for help amid the sex had the sound of their murders drowned out by other screams, drumbeats and clashing cymbals.*
> Livy, *History of Rome* 39.8ff

Rome, indeed all of Italy, was gripped by a moral panic in which neighbour looked at neighbour, each suspecting the other of participating in unspeakable vice and simultaneously fearing that they themselves would be falsely accused and thrown to an unreasoning mob looking for 'justice'. To all this the government added the weight of authority, not least because it was feared that so many aristocrats had been corrupted by Bacchus that they formed a 'second state'. The cult of Bacchus was considered a 'conspiracy' and priests and worshipers were hunted down and executed – with women handed over to their families for private (but equally severe) punishment.

below left
Attributed to Asteas, red-figure bell krater with Dionysus and comic actor, 360–340 BC.

below right
Attributed to the Choregos Painter, red-figure bell krater with bust of Dionysus and satyrs, c. 390–380 BC.
—
Satyrs were usually depicted as elderly, often bald with bulging bellies and long dangling genitals (which the ancient Greeks considered ugly). This is in marked contrast to the youthful, androgynous Dionysus.

left

Terracotta plaque with Bacchic worshipers, Roman, 27 BC–AD 68.

–

This Roman stele shows dancers in a Bacchic revel (note the panther skin at the waist of the male dancer). Despite the prim disapproval of the authorities, Bacchus remained popular, as attested by numerous sculptures and bas-reliefs showing parties and processions celebrating the god.

Yet despite this, the Romans were also aware that Bacchus himself was capable of smiting those who offended him too deeply, so they ensured that the god's shrines were not desecrated and those who applied to the authorities were still free to worship Bacchus, but in a restrained and dignified fashion.

The reformed Bacchanalia so closely followed the rites to the Roman god Liber that soon Bacchus and Liber were considered identical for all practical purposes. Exactly what their rites involved remains something of a mystery, as it was not a topic that the Romans were particularly inclined to discuss. It also seems reasonably clear from the archaeological evidence that, in southern Italy at least, men and women continued to meet in groups and drink wine after dark – without their communities collapsing into the debauched anarchy imagined by Livy (who was from Padua, a city in northern Italy that even the Romans considered somewhat uptight).

In Rome, Bacchus the wine god eventually became an established figure, particularly during the more relaxed era of the early Roman Empire. Since Bacchus embodied the spirit of the wine, the Romans could hardly abandon one without losing the other.

opposite

Fresco with Bacchus, from House of the Centenary, Pompeii, 1st century AD.

–

Bacchus stands beside what may be Mount Vesuvius, with his identifying thyrsus and panther. The bulbous items worn by Bacchus are unidentified but have been interpreted by some as grapes. The snake Agathodaemon was a benevolent protector of vineyards and cornfields.

HEPHAESTUS
⚔ VULCAN

Hollowed out by the Cyclopean furnaces,
the caverns of Etna resound with the echoes
from heavy blows to the anvils.
Piles of [cooling] Chalybean steel hiss in the caverns,
and fire roars through the furnaces.
This is Vulcan's home.

Virgil, *Aeneid* 8.419

The Greek myth of Hephaestus contains what academics call a 'chronological dichotomy' – a situation where something has gone very wrong with the timeline. The problem lies with the story of the birth of Hephaestus. In the most common form of the myth, Hephaestus was born because Hera was (as usual) somewhat miffed with her husband Zeus. In this case her annoyance was occasioned by the fact that Zeus had given birth to the goddess Athena, who had sprung, fully grown and perfect, from his forehead.

From Hera's point of view this made her somewhat redundant as a wife, especially as her union with Zeus had produced only one other Olympian god – the less-than-inspiring Ares. That Zeus on his own could have produced a deity such as Athena – superior to Ares in almost every way – Hera regarded as an insult to womankind in general and herself in particular. Therefore she decided to beat Zeus at his own game and produce a child by parthenogenesis – the process by which a female produces a child without male participation in the process.

In due course a child was born to her – but sadly he certainly did not have the body of a Greek god, even though he was one.

Pietro Tenerani, *Vulcan*, 1844.
–
This Neoclassical marble statue of the god shows him propped up on a crutch while clutching the hammer, which is a symbol of his status as a craftsman.

In fact, Hera took one look at the ugly child and in disgust tossed the babe from Olympus. Baby Hephaestus fell a very long way, before finally smacking into the Aegean Sea with such force that his leg was comprehensively broken – to the extent that even his godly powers could not restore him. Thus was born the legend of the lame craftsman god.

The problem with this story goes back to the birth of Athena (see p. 116) where it will be remembered that the labour pains of Zeus consisted of a truly monumental headache which was only relieved when his head was split open with an axe and Athena emerged. That axe, the myth informs us, was wielded by none other than Hephaestus, who was therefore not merely a prodigious child, as was Hermes, but capable of assisting the king of the gods in childbirth well before his own conception.

Those telling the myth did have one ready answer: as described in the introduction, the early cosmos was a mess and chaos reigned until the gods had put everything in order. This meant that tomorrow did not necessarily follow today, but could take place several years ago, as seems to have happened here. This was no great problem for the gods, who were outside time in any case, and who would have been no more perturbed by this development than a modern cinema-goer would be by a flashback scene in a movie.

Looking at things from a modern anthropological perspective, it is certainly true that Hephaestus was born in a time of chaos – those dark ages between the collapse of Mycenaean Greece and the dawn of the classical era. It is significant that Hephaestus was lame because many craftsmen of the Bronze Age were also. The reason is that bronze is an amalgam of copper and tin, and to make it more rigid blacksmiths would add arsenic, especially if supplies of tin were lacking as they often were, given that the stuff had to be imported along trade routes from as far away as Britain. Many Bronze Age blacksmiths were disabled due to long-term arsenic poisoning. However, we know that Hephaestus was an Iron Age god, so his lameness was retro-fitted to the myth to be consistent with a lingering popular belief of how a blacksmith should be.

Another reason for Hephaestus' ungodlike body was because he was a craftsman, and the Greek myth-makers were total snobs. Ordinary people seldom get even bit parts in the myths, which are almost exclusively taken up with the deeds of noblemen and deities. It was quite a feat for a god who specialized in something so common as manual labour to even muscle his way into the divine pantheon, but if he must be there,

Pieter van Aelst, Vulcan, detail from *The Honours* series of tapestries, *c.* 1523. Based on cartoons from the circle of Bernard van Orley and Jean Gossaert de Mabuse.

–

A hale and hearty-seeming Vulcan pounds dramatically on an anvil with the iron heated by multiple sets of bellows in this scene on a tapestry woven to celebrate the elevation of the Holy Roman Emperor Charles of Habsburg.

The Next Generation

then his physical imperfection should be in clear contrast to the noble beauty of his social superiors. Indeed, once established in the divine pantheon, Hephaestus spent his mythological career banging out armour and weaponry in the service of gods and high-born heroes.

Nevertheless, the problem with the craftsman god was that he was too talented and too cunning to be shoved to the back and ignored. After his fall into the ocean, he was found and adopted by the Nereid (sea nymph) Thetis, who is better known in later myths as the mother of the mighty Achilles. Even as an infant Hephaestus was fascinated by fire, and he found a way to maintain one even in an undersea forge. So beautiful was the jewelry that the grateful Hephaestus forged for Thetis that she was the subject of envious attention on her next visit to Olympus. Once enquiries had established that the maker of these exquisite ornaments was none other than her discarded child, Hera graciously extended an invitation to her son to visit her on Olympus.

opposite

Giuseppe Cesari,
Venus and Cupid in the Forge
of Vulcan, **17th century.**

—

This theme has been essayed
by artists from ancient Greece
to the modern era, perhaps
because of the contrast
between the beautiful,
aristocratic Venus, and the
sinewy musculature of the
craftsman god (who in this
picture looks considerably older
than Venus, his mother). The
occasion is presumably when
Venus prevails upon Vulcan to
craft armour for her warrior son
Aeneas.

Hephaestus replied that he felt unworthy of the honour and
would remain where he was, but as thanks for the invitation
he sent Hera a magnificent golden throne. When Hera
sat herself upon Hephaestus' gift, the weight of her divine
buttocks triggered the release of fine coils of wire which sprang
from the frame of the throne and entwined about Hera so
comprehensively that she could barely move a muscle. Apart
from Athena the many gods on Olympus were sadly lacking
in technical expertise, and Athena herself either couldn't or
wouldn't help (she liked Hephaestus and was no fan of her
step-mother). A stern demand from Zeus that Hephaestus
immediately release his mother received the icy reply, 'I have
no mother.'

Finally, Dionysus was prevailed upon to visit his half-brother
and ply him with wine. Then the wine-fuddled craftsman god
was hauled to Olympus (a popular theme often painted on
wine cups) where Zeus asked his terms for releasing Hera.
Hephaestus asked for the hand of Aphrodite in marriage –
a demand both reasonable and unreasonable, for while
craftsmanship and beauty go hand in hand, Hephaestus fell well

right

Attributed to the Foundry
Painter, red-figure kylix,
Hephaestus presents
Achilles' new armour to
Thetis, Greek, 5th century BC.

—

Thetis, the mother of Achilles,
picks up the armour that she
requested from Hephaestus.
The previous set was lost when
Patroclus used it to impersonate
Achilles and was slain on the
battlefield.

below the standard of physical beauty set by the other Olympian gods. Therefore, to demand marriage to the goddess of love was ambitious to say the least. However, Zeus was already looking to marry off his aunt, whose unattached status was causing problems among the perpetually over-sexed male inhabitants of Olympus, so he agreed to Hephaestus' demand.

The marriage was not a success, not least because (as was usual in ancient Greece) no one had consulted the bride about her preferences, and Aphrodite was not happy. She much preferred the macho battle god Ares and – forgetting about Hephaestus' cunning coils of wire – had an affair with him anyway. Inevitably her infidelity was discovered, and one day when Aphrodite and Ares buckled down to some serious adultery on one of her husband's couches, the coils of wire whipped out and imprisoned the pair *in flagrante delicto*. Hephaestus then strolled in accompanied by the other gods whom he had invited to view his tableau of humiliation. When everyone had laughed their fill, Hephaestus left Olympus to take up residence under Mount Etna in Sicily, becoming for all practical purposes divorced from his straying wife.

Maerten van Heemskerck, *Vulcan Showing the Captured Mars and Venus to the Gods*, c. 1540.

–

A depiction of the scene where Mars and Venus were caught *in flagrante delicto* by a cunning trap set by Vulcan, which ensnared the pair together on a couch. Vulcan then exhibited the adulterous couple to the other Olympian gods.

It was Mount Etna that provided a link by which the Romans connected one of their gods – a long-established deity called Volcanus – with Hephaestus. The original link was somewhat tenuous, for while Hephaestus was the god of craft and handiwork, Volcanus – later named Vulcan – was the god of wildfire. While people mostly pray for what their gods can do for them, the Romans prayed to Vulcan so that he would not do anything. In an afternoon, wildfire could undo a season's work in a grain field, devastate a warehouse, or if it poured from a volcano, wipe out an entire city.

It was no coincidence that most of the celebrations honouring Vulcan took place towards the end of summer when the fields and forests were at their driest and the risk of devastating fires was most acute. The various rites culminated in the Vulcanalia celebrations of 23 August, with events and sacrifices, including the lighting of a fire. A small animal or fish was thrown into the flames, perhaps as an echo of a more barbaric era when the sacrificial victim was human.

The Romans avoided building shrines to Vulcan within the city limits, for the same reason that one does not invite a pyromaniac into a firework factory. Where Rome's city limits gradually expanded beyond long-standing edifices dedicated to Vulcan (he was a very ancient god), the Romans had decided that the risk of moving the god outweighed the dangers of leaving him be, and the places of worship remained. One of these was quite close to the Roman Forum, where it was said to have been established by King Titus Tatius in the very early days when Rome was still a fortress settlement on the Palatine Hill.

Early statues of Vulcan show a robust and able-bodied being, often with a hammer in one hand, for the Etruscans were the first to identify Vulcan with Hephaestus and passed the craftsman attribute on to the Romans, who later completed the process of Greekification by making Vulcan lame. Thereafter legend says that Vulcan got about in a chair with wheels – a useful device that disabled mortals of the classical era do not seem to have imitated.

Apart from a common interest in volcanoes (which are named after Vulcan rather than the other way around), the factor uniting Hephaestus and Vulcan was fire. Hephaestus was said to have been fascinated by fire and did his best work in a smithy. Vulcan was a fire god, so merging him with Hephaestus involved taking his fire from the woods and cornfields and putting it to use in metalwork. After this conflation we see

Vulcan making a magnificent shield for Aeneas, the father of the Roman people, just as Hephaestus made similar shields for Heracles and Achilles. All three shields are described with loving detail by the poets, to the point where the number of scenes described meant that either the images on the shields were microscopically small, or the shields could have roofed a small building.

If the Romans kept Vulcan at arm's length, the practically minded Athenians made Hephaestus more welcome in their city than anywhere else in the Greek world apart from the god's favoured island of Lemnos. According to legend, Hephaestus counted as the father of the Athenians, albeit somewhat by accident. The god often worked closely with Athena, since in her aspect of Athena *Ergane* ('Athena of crafts') the two gods had much in common. When Athena was putting together the geography of what was to become her favoured city of Athens, Hephaestus decided it was time to make his move.

Athena was carrying a mass of earth and rock intended to enlarge the hill upon which the later Acropolis would stand when Hephaestus launched his clumsy attempt at seduction. The startled goddess dropped what she was carrying (which became the crooked mini-mountain known today as Lycabettus) and leapt away, but not before Hephaestus had ejaculated onto her thigh.

This Athena wiped away with a skein of wool and the fallen semen fell to the earth, from which sprang Erichthonius (from *erion* 'wool' + *cthonos* 'earth'), who was to the Athenians as Aeneas was to the Romans – the founder of their race. Thus Hephaestus was given a splendid temple on the north-west side of the Athenian agora, and since one has to build a temple to a craftsman god with the finest attention to detail, the well-constructed edifice has weathered the ages to stand largely intact today.

Vulcan is also credited with fathering Caeculus, the legendary founder of the Italian city of Praeneste (today Palestrina). He was conceived more conventionally by Vulcan – or at least as conventionally as divine conceptions go. Legend has it that the mother of Caeculus was lying by the fire when a spark leapt from the flames to her womb. (Exactly what the lady was doing at the fireside to make this possible beggars the imagination.) Another result of this fiery conception was that Vulcan became the patron god of one of Rome's great families, for a descendant of Caeculus moved to Rome to found the line of the Caecilii Metelli.

Paris Bordone, *Athena Scorning the Advances of Hephaestus*, c. 1555–60.

–

Athena and the craftsman god worked closely together in constructing the physical location of Athens. The virgin goddess intended the relationship to be strictly business but Hephaestus had other ideas in mind.

The Next Generation

While the volcanoes of Vulcan were justly feared, they bestowed two great gifts upon the Romans. Firstly, volcanic soil was so famously rich that Vulcan was also considered a fertility god. Secondly, volcanic ash produced pozzolana, which was the basis of Roman concrete. This was often of higher quality than the modern version: for example, the hydraulic concrete piers at the seaport of Cosa remain in excellent condition despite having been underwater for 2,000 years.

BEYOND OLYMPUS

Janus

Hecate ⚔ Trivia

Hestia ⚔ Vesta

Isis ⚔ Serapis

Asclepius ⚔ Aesculapius

Mithras

'Belief systems' are defined by anthropologists as being in part concerned with the existence of certain conceptual entities, such as gods. A society can be polytheistic but have a single belief system. For example, Hinduism contains multiple gods, but is the only religion practised in some parts of India. The Romans were not only polytheistic but also accepting of multiple belief systems, the Greeks less so.

In classical Greece the Gods who were not a part of the Olympic pantheon greatly outnumbered those who were, since the number of Olympian gods was set at twelve. Thus, when Dionysus forced his way to the top table on Mount Olympus, another god had to step down. Usually this was Hestia, goddess of the hearth – but not always. There were some regional variations in opinion as to who constituted the twelve Olympian gods. For example, sometimes Hades was counted as a member of a separate pantheon – that of the Chthonic gods – and not as an Olympian, particularly as Mount Olympus was a place he seldom, if ever, visited. However, Olympian or not, most of the gods of Greece were incorporated within the same belief system, and the myths have minor gods such as Pan interacting with the greater gods within the same mythological framework and belief system.

In ancient Rome the religious picture was considerably more diverse because the Romans were considerably more diverse. To be a Greek was a matter of culture – it was something of a subjective opinion whether someone was Greek or not. The Macedonians, for example, felt very strongly that they were Greek, but the southern Greeks somewhat contemptuously rejected that claim until Philip II, father of Alexander the Great, forced them to agree at sword-point. Since a Greek was by definition one who subscribed to Greek cultural norms, Greeks tended to follow the same religion.

On the other hand, being Roman was a legal definition of one's civic status, in the same way that 'Greeks' were actually Athenians, Thebans or Neapolitans. (Naples, from Nea Polis, meaning 'new city', was Greek for the first thousand years of its existence. In fact, because Greek was a cultural definition and Roman a legal one, there was nothing stopping people from being Greek Romans, and many were.) So, we had Romans

Fresco with Isis Fortuna, from Caupona of Tertius, Pompeii, 1st century AD.

—

Isis, the ancient Egyptian goddess, was adopted across the Roman Empire. Here she is combined with the Roman goddess Fortuna. On the left, two snakes – symbols of protection – tower over a nude, squatting man.

practising the Greek form of religion, and other Romans who worshiped Babylonian, Phoenician, Jewish and Gallic gods among a host of others.

This was not a problem for the Romans because, while their people had multiple belief systems, they had a single state religion. Roman religion was based upon the Greco-Roman gods, but the *Pax Deorum* – the agreement between the Roman state and its gods – did not forbid the worship of other deities as well, so long as that worship was done privately and not as a part of official civic ritual. (Nevertheless, that 'as well' caused considerable tension with the monotheistic Jews, and later a great deal more with the aggressively monotheistic Christians.) A good analogy today might be how modern state authorities demand that citizens pay their taxes to the state but have no objections to people contributing money to other social causes as well.

Therefore, when we define the gods of Rome, we actually need two definitions – there were the gods worshiped by Rome as a state and gods worshiped by the Romans as a people. In this section we look at examples of three types of god: non-Olympian gods who were worshiped in Greece and Rome, namely Aesculapius, Hecate and Pan; gods who were part of the Roman belief system, Janus and the Magna Mater; and gods worshiped in Rome who were not a part of the Greco-Roman belief system, Isis and Mithras, who were nevertheless deeply embedded in Roman society.

JANUS

The statue of two-faced Janus, dedicated by King Numa,
is worshiped as a symbol of war and peace, the fingers of the statue
being so arranged as to indicate the days of the year,
and to show that Janus is a god of time.

Pliny the Elder, *Natural History* 34.16

Today we know Janus from January; he is the god of beginnings who has given his name to the opening month of the year. Yet to the Romans Janus was so much more. Firstly, Janus was not only the god of beginnings but also the god of endings. When an infant became a child, Janus was there, and again at childhood's end when a girl became a woman, and a boy became a man. Any transition in human or natural conditions required Janus, the divine agency without whom nothing could change from one state to another.

For the Romans Janus was the oldest of gods, for Janus the god of beginnings was born as soon as the universe came into existence. In fact, with his dual nature, Janus is the divine bookends of eternity, for once the universe finally runs down and everything has gone, it is Janus the god of endings who, metaphorically speaking, will sweep up the floor and turn off the lights.

Janus is so old a god that it is uncertain whether he gets his name for the ancient word for 'portal' (in other words a doorway or a gateway) or whether the word comes from the god. (His name survives today with the modern custodian of such portals, the janitor.) The role of portals is intimately connected with

Head of Janus, Etruscan, 1st century BC.

—

This sculpture comes from Etruria, home of the Etruscans. At this time, Etruscan culture and language were becoming so permeated by Roman culture that the adoption of this uniquely Roman god would have caused little comment.

Glass cup with head of Janus, Roman, 1st century AD.

–

A youthful-seeming Janus looks both ways on this glass Roman drinking vessel.

Janus because as one enters or leaves a building, especially one's home, this marks a transition to a different set of circumstances. To a Roman, leaving through the city gates meant transitioning from the (relative) safety of the city to the perils of the outside world.

Janus was a portal in another way also: no Roman invoked his gods without first invoking Janus, for he was the intermediary between human and divine. Therefore, Roman religious ceremonies invariably began with a prayer to Janus 'the creator and parent of our years', as the poet Martial calls him. These ceremonies ended, incidentally, with a prayer to Vesta, the divine mother-guardian of the Roman state.

Janus also reveals a difference between the cultures of Rome and Greece when it came to religion. The Greek gods were essentially forces, be they the power of love, order or growth. These forces had a rational human-facing aspect, which not only could interact with humans but which also shared the human experience with their loves, feuds and personal tragedy. For the Romans their 'gods' were concepts, usually the perfect embodiment of a thing or an idea. Unlike the Greeks, the early Romans felt little need to humanize their gods, and while they later happily adopted the Greek myths wholesale, they felt little need to add a human backstory to their own divinities.

Furthermore, while Roman belief systems certainly coloured how the Greeks approached their gods, especially in the Roman imperial period, the Greeks saw neither a way to incorporate gods such as Janus into their own theology (beginnings and endings are concepts, but certainly not forces) nor any need to do so.

As a result, Janus is shut out of the Greco-Roman myths and has no detailed biography of his own. A relationship with Cardea (the goddess of hinges and heart valves) was natural enough given the importance of hinges to gates and doors, but more intriguing is the idea that for a while Janus was king of a tribe of early Italians called the Aborigines, from whom the term 'aboriginal' originates.

This has led to the consideration that the original Janus might have been a prehistoric king of sufficient stature that beliefs accumulated about him, each growing in improbability until his actions could only be explained by a divine nature. (The Romans – who were refreshingly undogmatic about their religion – also speculated that this might be the case.) It may be that any undertaking by the Aborigines started by invoking the memory of their late king, and things developed from there, until we reach the point where Cato the Elder judiciously advises farmers:

> [Before starting the harvest] make an offering of cakes to Janus saying these words: 'Father Janus, in offering these cakes, I humbly beg that you will bestow grace and mercy on me, my children, and my household.'
> Cato, *De Agricultura* 134

Critical as the harvest was, this was among the lesser responsibilities of Janus. It was he whom the Romans first invoked upon the making of peace and the declaration of war. One of the few myths relating to the god comes from the very early days of Rome, when the indignant Sabines were fighting to reclaim their daughters whom the Romans, wanting wives, had abducted. The Romans were pushed back to the

above
Didrachm depicting Janus, Roman, c. 215 BC.

—

This Roman silver didrachm was struck during the Punic war against Hannibal and was probably used for legionary pay. It shows Janus on one side and on the other Jupiter driving a four-horse chariot while at his shoulder the indistinct shape of Victory urges him on.

opposite
Miniature with Janus, 15th century.

—

Even in the Christian era, the duality of Janus made the god a useful allegorical figure. Here he looks on one side to peace, where we see a knight doffing his chainmail, and on the other to war, with cavalry riding into battle.

city gate and closed it as they retreated. However, the gates mysteriously re-opened and the Sabines came storming in, only to be swept away by a boiling spring which spontaneously erupted from the temple of Janus.

From there onward it was decreed that when Rome was at war the gates of the 'temple' (which was more of an arched passageway) should stand open so that the god could more easily exit to help his people. In times of peace the gates were closed, which might have required the liberal use of oil, since during the long history of the Roman Republic the gates were only closed twice.

The Romans also attributed to Janus the invention of coinage and numerous coins were struck depicting the two faces of the god. We also have coins from the imperial era which show Janus more completely as a tall, bearded man with two faces (or four, as he is sometimes shown facing each of the cardinal directions). He is shown with a staff, because he guides travellers at the start of their journey, and a key because portals are sometimes locked, and Janus represents the way through.

Finally, it is a suitable tribute to this enigmatic god that the greatest of his surviving monuments in Rome – the Arch of Janus – may have nothing to do with the god after all. However, little is known about the reasons for the building of this odd structure. This is a quadrifrons arch and the fact that it has four faces led to the belief that this was a monument to the (sometimes) four-faced god, and a reminder that, as with the four seasons, the beginning of one thing marks the ending of another.

HECATE
✕✕
TRIVIA

Hecate! Carrier of torches, daughter sprung from the loins of black Night.

Bacchylides, Ep 2. *Ode To Hecate*

Many today are familiar with Hecate as the spirit summoned by the witches in Shakespeare's *Macbeth* – a malevolent entity, 'the close contriver of all harms', who intends to contrive magicks which will blind Macbeth to the fatal consequences of his actions. From our point of view, it is interesting that a Greek goddess should appear at all in a play dealing with eleventh-century Scottish politics.

The reason is that, as a goddess, Hecate was remarkably hard to kill. Over a millennium after western Europe had become officially Christian, there were still folk who sacrificed to the goddess of the crossroads, and the Church had responded by using character assassination to exorcise this most persistent of pagan deities from the minds of its flock.

The Christian churchmen were not the only religious authorities to have issues with Hecate. She was a problem from the get-go, when her worship first spread to Greece, probably from Asia Minor. There Hecate was a major goddess, a mother-figure who appears to have been particularly associated with the moon and wild things. While etymologists have struggled to find the source of her name, the most likely explanation is that Hecate means 'she who works from afar'.

Marble statuette of a triple-bodied Hecate, Roman, 1st–2nd century AD.
–
This statuette shows the goddess with her iconic torches. In her Roman form Hecate was Trivia, goddess of the crossroads. A Roman crossroads was what we would call today a 'T-junction'.

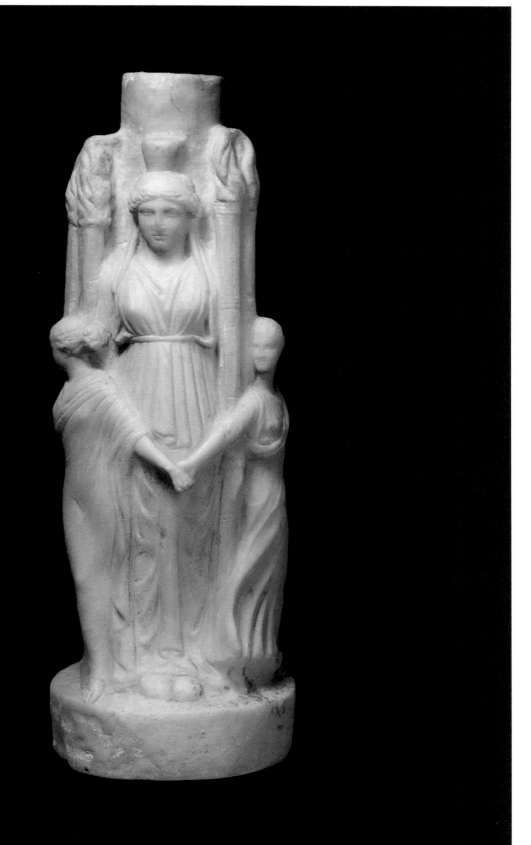

Once Hecate had reached Greece, Greek theologians had to decide what to make of her. The usual process of syncretism did not work for Hecate, who combined aspects of Hera, Selene (goddess of the moon) and Artemis. (It is possible that Hecate did return to Asia Minor as Artemis, for in Asia Minor Artemis adopted many of the attributes that Hecate had there originally.) A further attribute of Hecate, and the one that made her worship particularly persistent, was that she was seen as a protector of the underdog – and the ancient and medieval world had an awful lot of underdogs. Because she had so many Greek worshipers, Hecate could not just be ignored or wished away – a place had to be found for her within the religious framework.

It did not make things any easier that Hecate was a powerful goddess who was given careful respect by both mortals and gods. The poet Hesiod called the goddess 'she to whom even mighty Zeus affords due honour'. We also see this in another way – while even senior deities such as Demeter might be raped by male gods, and Athena and Artemis had to exert themselves on occasion to protect their virginity, no one messed with Hecate.

One of the myths that helped define Hecate comes from the rape of Demeter. At the time Demeter was searching for her missing daughter Persephone. The other gods suspected that Zeus had been complicit in the kidnapping and gave Demeter no help whatsoever – and her brother Poseidon raped her. Up stepped Hecate, goddess of the underdog, who helped Demeter in her search, even leading the way into the underworld to confront grim Hades. (For this reason, Hecate is often shown carrying two torches – one for herself and one for Demeter as the pair proceeded into the shadows below.)

As was generally the case when she intervened in the affairs of the great gods, Hecate went unpunished. In fact, the great gods carefully pretended that the intervention had not happened at all. Yet in this case Hecate's trip to the underworld gave her a role whereby she could fit into the Greek theological system. She became a goddess of the underworld – indeed after Persephone she was *the* goddess of the underworld, and even more so because Persephone drew her power from her position as the wife of Hades, while Hecate stood alone. Neither myth nor those who called upon Hecate ever imply that she needed to seek permission from Hades before acting.

This combination of protector of the underdog and mistress of dark powers is one reason why we know so much about Hecate. In both Greece and Rome those who felt ill done by but

Lamp in the form of a bust
of Hecate, Greek,
2nd–1st century BC.

—

A painted terracotta lamp
depicting a crowned Hecate
holding a torch. The body of the
torch is designed to be filled
with oil with the wick emerging
at the end, thus allowing Hecate
her traditional role of bringing
light to dark places.

powerless to take revenge often resorted to curse tablets. These little tablets, usually taking the form of carefully inscribed and folded lead strips, called on particular deities to blight the life of the person being cursed, often in particularly imaginative and very comprehensive ways. Hecate was a favourite among the gods called upon to do the deed.

One such tablet was found in the grave of a young Athenian woman. It calls on Hermes, Artemis and Hecate to 'throw their hatred' upon the writer's enemies, their persons and their businesses, and to 'bind them with the dead in blood and ashes'. Here we see again the connection between Artemis and Hecate, and we should not be surprised to see Hermes getting involved. He was the god of those businesses that were being cursed to fail, but he is also mentioned because while meeting the young woman to guide her spirit to the underworld it was Hermes who would have picked up the message left buried in her grave.

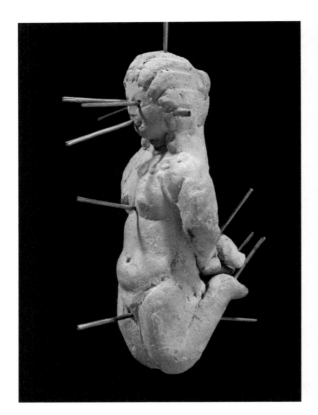

The Romans believed that one way to be cured of an illness was to be rubbed all over with a puppy, for Hecate had a connection with dogs, even though mortal hounds tended to howl and try to burrow their way inside under the door when she walked abroad. Hecate's familiars were a large black dog and a weasel. The black dog was formerly Hecuba, wife of Priam of Troy. Hecuba had left her young children in the safekeeping of a distant king at the start of the Trojan War. When he heard that Troy had fallen, he killed the children, not realizing that Hecuba would return for them and be murderously upset when she learned of their fate. Standing over the dead king's body and fighting off his retainers like a mad dog, Hecuba was saved by Hecate, who transformed Hecuba into the killer hound that she seemed to be.

The weasel was a later addition – a nurse incurred Hera's wrath by assisting with the birth of Heracles and was transformed into this beast. Again, Hecate stepped in and made the former nurse part of her entourage. In later years many

above left
Magic figurine, Roman, from Egypt, 3rd–4th century AD.

above right
Tablet with an incantation against epilepsy, Roman, 3rd century AD.

—

Hecate was often invoked in curse spells, which were often graphically illustrated as with this doll probably used in a binding spell. The woman's sense organs, heart and genitals are pierced with pins. Less frequently Hecate was invoked as a healer, as in this thin gold strip inscribed with a spell against epilepsy. (Poorer people used lead strips when sending messages to the goddess.)

Drawen by Mr Cosway

This Figure has
in the other Hand
a burning Torch

I write you and you a drawing of the other side of this Siren if this comes all out of your Paper — I wish to keep your illustration a Serg on this long if you have no Objection) as I feel I have gained much information from it

R. Cosway. del.

left
Triple head of Hecate, fragment of a statue, Asia Minor, 2nd–3rd century AD.
–
This fragment of a statue of the goddess shows one head wearing a floral wreath while the others have turreted crowns – often a symbol of divine protection in times of war.

households in Greece and Rome kept a weasel on the premises, both for pest control and as a gesture of respect to Hecate.

The crossroads were an important place, symbolically speaking – they were where one path in life met another and led in new directions. Hecate liked to meet her worshipers there, especially pregnant women looking for blessings for their unborn child. (In later eras the Christian Church got very annoyed about this.) Because a crossroads in the classical era was what we would today call a T-junction, Hecate became a tripartite deity – a goddess with three bodies who in later traditions of witchcraft were a maiden, a mother and a crone, each facing in a different direction of the crossroads.

From here we get the Roman name for the goddess, Trivia: *tri* 'three' + *via* 'roads'. (The modern word 'trivia' – meaning disparate and unimportant facts – comes indirectly from the Latin for crossroads, and the gossip there exchanged, rather than from association with the goddess herself.) The Romans again called up the association with Diana and the moon so that the tripartite being of the crossroads manifested as the wild things of earth, a celestial being of the sky and a denizen of the

previous page
Richard Cosway, *Hecate Trimorph*, 1768–1805.
–
This sketch drawn from a marble original in pen and brown ink by artist Richard Cosway shows that modern fascination with the three-bodied goddess dates back at least to the early 1800s.

below

William Blake, *The Night of Enitharmon's Joy* (formerly called *Hecate*), c. 1795.

–

This illustration is rich in symbolism, with a central figure who may reference either the moon goddess in Shakespeare's *Midsummer Night's Dream* or Hecate's role in *Macbeth*. Her hand rests on a book of magic and she is accompanied by a crocodile (symbolizing hypocrisy), an ass and a bat with a cat's head.

underworld – in short a deity who encompassed most of the known universe. That Trivia was an all-encompassing god who existed in three persons was a feature that the later Christian Church considered thoroughly blasphemous to the Holy Trinity and it constituted a further reason why worship of Hecate was particularly frowned upon.

The association of Hecate with the underworld made it easy to link her to demons and witchcraft. Indeed, the association already existed in the pre-Christian era, though at that time Hecate's power over evil spirits was invoked to ask the goddess to bring them under control.

In recent years, with the growth of religions such as the Wiccan, worship of Hecate has come out of the shadows, and today the goddess has more professed worshipers than Jupiter, Apollo or all the Olympian gods combined.

HESTIA
⚹
VESTA

Most ancient goddess who lives within the eternal flame of the household fire…
In you we find the chosen dwelling of the gods and the strong,
stable foundation of humanity. Eternal queen, ever flowering
and changing, laughing, beautiful and blessed.

Orphic Hymn 84

In an average household in the classical world, kitchens were for the rich. Most people prepared their food right there in the living room, at the hearth. Here sat the large stove, fuelled by wood, around which family life was centred. As well as providing cooked food and warmth in winter, the hearth was a reliable source of flame for elsewhere in the household – highly important when heat and light came only from fire.

The oldest hearth ever found by archaeologists is over 300,000 years old and pre-dates the arrival of modern humans in the region where it was found. Given the centrality of the hearth to the household, it was inevitable that there would be a god of the hearth, and given the centrality of the matriarch to the household, it was inevitable that this deity be a goddess.

For the Greeks this goddess was Hestia and since the hearth was ancient well before the ancient Greeks, Hestia is generally considered the oldest of her generation – the elder sister of Zeus, Poseidon and Hades. Yet unlike her squabbling and fractious siblings, Hestia was quiet and unassuming – not a source of strife, but a refuge from it.

As humanity formed larger social groupings, the hearth and its goddess took on a wider significance – the sacred flame of

Hestia Giustiniani, Roman copy of Greek original (470–460 BC), 2nd century AD.
–
Hestia wears a Greek peplum and is modestly veiled. This particular statue is named after its owner Vincenzo Giustiniani, an early 17th-century collector of art and antiquities.

Hestia spread from the home to the town hall and became the symbolic fireside of the entire community. Hestia herself did not leave the home, where any social occasion began with the ritual pouring of wine (libation) to the goddess, but now she became to some degree also the mother-protector of a village, town or city.

According to Roman tradition, Hestia came to Italy with Aeneas, who also brought with him the traditional minor gods of the household, the *penates*. Yet this belief is almost certainly mistaken. Not only is the Roman version of the name – Vesta – so ancient that its meaning is lost (while we know that Hestia essentially means 'hearth' in Greek) but Vesta retains many of the attributes of a pre-Greek Roman deity. That is, there are precious few myths concerning the goddess, and she is more often portrayed as a flame than as an anthropomorphic deity. Roman legend claims that the worship of Vesta was institutionalized in Rome by its second king, Numa, but her worship went back much further than that.

Most early Iron Age communities had a goddess like Vesta and it appears that at least some had the tradition that the sacred fire was tended by virgin priestesses. (Given the difficulty involved in lighting a fire from scratch it is understandable that a community wanted to have at least one fire always burning.)

Hanging with Hestia Polyolbus ('Hestia of many blessings'), Byzantine, 6th century AD.

—

This tapestry shows a crowned Hestia surrounded by genii who each hold a disc proclaiming the gifts of good cheer, wealth, fortune prosperity and mirth. The crowned figures on the right and left may symbolize light and love.

Giovanni Battista Piranesi, sketch of imaginary ancient temple in honour of Vesta, 1743.

—

Not content with the shrine Vesta actually had in Rome, Piranesi imagined a more splendid building (modelled on the Pantheon) with a large altar in the centre in the contemporary Neoclassical style.

Certainly this was the case in the now-vanished city of Alba Longa, where one of the priestesses of Vesta was Rhea Silvia, the mother of Romulus and Remus (see p. 27).

In Rome the Vestal Virgins were charged with keeping the sacred flame of Vesta always burning in her shrine. Vesta did not have a temple because a Roman temple was defined as a place where a type of priest called an augur could take the auspices to determine the will of the gods (which gave to posterity words such as 'inaugurate' and 'auspicious'). Since augurs were male and the Roman home of Vesta was for females only, it followed that the shrine of Vesta could not be a temple.

PLACATUS MITISQUE ROGANT ISMENIDES ADSIS ·

There certainly was a male presence within Vesta's shrine, and a rather baffling one at that. The Romans – and Greeks – believed that looks could literally kill and made strenuous attempts to ward off the Evil Eye. They did this with the aid of a god called Fascinus, who took the form of a large, erect phallus. The keeper of this phallus was the goddess Vesta and her virginal attendants had the constant presence of Fascinus in their shrine to remind them of what they were missing.

Certainly being a Vestal Virgin had its compensations – Vestals were chosen from the most aristocratic families in Rome and were immediately freed from the authority of their fathers. Vestals got front row seats at the amphitheatre and could immediately free any prisoner should they so wish. Because they were protected by the goddess, the blood of Vestals could not be spilled even if they broke their most sacred oath of chastity. Instead, their fate was much worse – a straying Vestal was ritually sealed alive within the city walls and left there to die alone in darkness.

Rome left the protection of Vesta in AD 394, when the cult was banned by the Christian emperor Theodosius. Sixteen years later the city was sacked by the Visigoths.

While Vesta was always one of the *Dii Consentes* – the Roman version of the Olympian gods – Hestia herself was not always one of the twelve. Laid-back and unassuming, in many traditions she was reckoned to have given up her place to the pushy, young, up-and-coming god Dionysus. Other cities, however, reckoned her still as one of the Olympians, preferring the peace of the hearth to the wild ructions of the party god.

opposite
Agostino Comerio, *Vestals*, from Palazzo Maffei, Verona, 1817.

–

A depiction of rather raucous Roman women playing music and dancing as they tend to Vesta's sacred flame.

right
Jean-Baptiste Peytavin, *Le Supplice d'une vestale*, before 1801.

–

The fate of a Vestal who broke her vows was to be entombed alive within the city walls of Rome – her male lover was flogged and then executed. Over the centuries fewer than a dozen Vestals suffered this punishment.

ISIS

She that is the natural mother of all things, the leader and controller
of all elemental forces, the mistress of everything supernatural,
the queen of heaven and the gods above, the light of the [other] goddesses,
who commands the planets in the sky, the winds of the ocean,
and the silence of the underworld. A name, a godhood adored
throughout all the world.

Apuleius, *The Golden Ass*

Statuette of Isis nursing Horus, Egyptian, 664–332 BC.

–

Isis had a role as protective mother – one common to many religions. Her son Horus was a sky god (his name is derived from the word for 'falcon') and he and Isis came to be associated with the person of the pharaoh.

That 'name adored through all the world' was that of the goddess Isis. While that name has recently been linked to fanaticism and terrorism in the popular imagination, doubtless Isis will outlive the insult. She has, after all, been worshiped as a goddess for some 4,500 years.

Isis appears to have first been worshiped by the Egyptians of the Fifth Dynasty (*c.* 2500–2300 BC), roughly a thousand years before the first civilizations in Greece. Yet at this point, though a major goddess in Egypt, Isis had very few worshipers elsewhere – a condition that remained so until the Macedonian ruler Alexander the Great conquered Egypt in 332 BC.

The conquests of Alexander expanded the Hellenistic world from the shores of the Aegean Sea right across the former Persian Empire all the way to the mountains of present-day Afghanistan. Yet even as the Greeks spread their culture eastward (it is possible to see Greek influences even in the art of the contemporary Mauryan Empire of India), the influence of other cultures was seeping into their own.

Among these foreign influences was the worship of Isis, which was spread both by converted Greeks in Egypt and by Egyptians moving abroad to settle elsewhere in the new, cosmopolitan

Fresco with Isis receiving Io, from the Temple of Isis, Pompeii, 1st century AD.

—

This fresco shows Isis with a cobra (here symbolizing royal wisdom) welcoming the nymph Io (left) to Egypt. Isis wears Roman dress, while Io still has heifer's horns on her head. She is carried by a male figure who is probably a personification of the Nile.

Hellenistic world. One way we can see how her religion spread is by contemporary epithets, which talk of 'Isis of the waves' and 'Isis of Pharos'. (Pharos was the island on which the Great Lighthouse of Alexandria was built.) Thus we see, for example, Isis of the Nile becoming the goddess of those merchants and seafarers who made landfall on the Greek island of Delos, and soon afterwards shrines and temples to Isis became established in Greek cities from Iran to Italy.

The acceptance of Isis outside Egypt was helped along by the fact that unlike many Egyptian gods she had a human rather than an animal head. It also helped that the Greeks saw Egyptian religion as ancient and powerful (if somewhat bizarre) and from Herodotus we know that the Greeks were well aware of how strongly Egyptian religious beliefs had coloured their own theology ('You Greeks are children', an Egyptian priest once told him). Thus Isis, although never welcomed into the Olympic pantheon, was adopted as a Greek-style goddess to the extent that her original priests probably would have been outraged at how Hellenized their goddess had become.

The Romans were considerably more reserved when they first met Isis in the second century BC. For a start, the worship of Isis was a mystery cult, a type of religion that the Romans regarded with deep suspicion. (A mystery cult is a religion that keeps secrets that are only known to initiates.) Nevertheless, as Rome took control of the Greek cities of southern Italy, it also took control of worshipers of Isis, who carried the worship of their goddess right into the heart of Rome itself.

This further unsettled the Roman authorities, who were accustomed to having control of their gods through priesthoods apportioned to Roman politicians and aristocrats. There seemed

Statuette of Isis-Aphrodite, Roman, 2nd century AD.

—

Since followers of Isis in Greco-Roman culture claimed that their goddess embodied all the female deities of the Olympic pantheon, it was possible for Egypt's Hellenistic queens to combine the majesty of Isis with the more flattering aspects of Aphrodite. This statuette probably once had a mirror in one hand and a flower in the other.

no way of incorporating Isis into the Roman pantheon, not least because her claims were so overwhelming. According to her worshipers, Isis was not just another goddess but the supreme deity, dominant over other gods – and particularly other goddesses, such as Juno and Minerva. Indeed, according to followers of her cult, these other goddesses might be considered simply as different aspects of great Isis herself.

In the Roman novel quoted at the beginning of the chapter, Isis makes these claims for herself also: 'The Athenians call me Artemis; the Cypriots, Aphrodite; the Sicilians, Proserpina of the Shadows; and the Eleusians call me Demeter. Some call me Juno,

Priest of Isis as Anubis, from the Temple of Isis, Pompeii, 1st century AD.

–

In this fresco a priest of Isis is mysteriously portrayed with the head of Anubis. Anubis was the Egyptian god of graves and cemeteries, a role played by Hermes in the Greek pantheon. He was fathered by Osiris, the husband of Isis in Egyptian myth.

Beyond Olympus

Fresco with cult of Isis, Herculaneum, 1st century AD.

—

This fresco shows a priest at the altar, with two sacred Egyptian ibises in the foreground and a Nubian retainer at the rear. The altar is decorated with garlands, and the seated figure is playing a sistrum (a type of percussion instrument).

others Bellona of the Battles, and yet others call me Hecate.' Isis, in other words, was the one goddess to rule them all.

The Romans, in their usual easy-going way with (most) other religions, cheerfully allowed Isis to make these claims and then largely disregarded them, although the emperor Augustus forbade the goddess places of worship within the city limits of Rome itself. Elsewhere in the empire things were more relaxed, and anyone who wants to visit a temple of Isis today can still step inside the largely intact temple in the former Roman port city of Ostia.

Worship of Isis largely disappeared when Rome became Christian, with many believers switching their faith to that of Mary, the virgin mother (whose early iconic pictures with the baby Jesus bear a suspicious resemblance to earlier depictions of Isis with her son Horus). Nevertheless, worship of Isis seems not so much to have completely disappeared as gone underground, and today numerous neo-pagan websites testify to renewed worship of the ancient goddess.

SERAPIS

One of the common people of Alexandria, well known for
his blindness, threw himself before [the emperor] Vespasian, begging
him for a cure. He had been told to do this by the god Serapis, whom this
most superstitious of nations worships above all others.

Tacitus, *Histories* 4.81

While the early Egyptians were comfortable enough with
a female goddess who had almost unchecked powers, the
strongly patriarchal Greeks were much less so. Therefore when
Ptolemy – the former general of Alexander the Great – took
power in Egypt, he set about bringing Isis under male control.
He did this by ordering up a consort for the goddess in the form
of a male counterpart, the new god Serapis.

For monotheists accustomed to one God, eternal and
unchanging, there is something startling about a head of
government deciding that his state needed a new god and
creating one accordingly. Yet within a religious system that saw
the gods as anthropomorphized forces and paradigms, this was
a relatively straightforward process. After all, scientists regularly
discover new elements and forces, such as dark matter and
quarks, so if the ancients saw a gap in their belief system they
were quite ready to adopt and deify that force once they had
identified it. And it was a truth universally acknowledged in the
Greco-Roman belief system that a single goddess in possession
of great powers must be in want of a husband.

Ptolemy had other reasons for bringing Serapis into being.
He was in a somewhat uncomfortable position as the Greek

**Marble head of Jupiter
Serapis, Roman,
2nd century AD.**

–

The *kalanthos* was a sacred
basket that carried fruits or
vegetables dedicated to a
god at religious ceremonies.
The presence of the *kalanthos*
identifies this sculpture as a
bust of Serapis (although here
only the head is ancient). The
face was originally painted red,
as was the face of Jupiter, so
this head is named 'the Jupiter
Serapis'.

Limestone stela with snake-bodied figures of Isis and Dionysus Serapis, Roman, 1st century BCE–1st century AD.

–

This peculiar combination of Roman heads and serpent bodies shows how Roman religion adapted different aspects of gods (and methods of depicting the gods) from across the Empire.

overlord of the Egyptian state. He was well aware that many Egyptians familiar with the long and proud history of their nation did not like foreign rulers one bit. They had already demonstrated this with frequent and enthusiastic rebellions against the Persian rulers whom the Greeks had supplanted. So Ptolemy tried to make himself more Egyptian, building temples to their gods, making himself pharaoh and ordering statues to be made of himself in traditional Egyptian dress.

Yet even as he strove to appear Egyptian to the Egyptians, Ptolemy wanted to appear Greek to the Greeks. It was after all only a single generation since Alexander the Great's father, Philip II of Macedon, had forced the Greeks at sword point to admit that their 'barbarian' northern neighbours were as Greek as they were. To help him straddle this rather uncomfortable fence with Greeks on one side and Egyptians on the other, Ptolemy created Serapis – a god who merged aspects of Greek and Egyptian religion into a single deity.

Just as Isis combined aspects of other Greek and Roman goddesses into her Hellenized self, Serapis took on aspects of the older Greek gods. Surviving statues show Serapis with iconography that is usually linked to Hades. This is because the somewhat sketchy foundation upon which Ptolemy's new god was built was the Apis bull – a bull believed to be a manifestation of the god Osiris, whom the Greeks considered to be the Egyptian version of Hades. When that bull died it was buried and became a divinity known as Osiris-apis, or – as Ptolemy preferred to call him – Serapis.

Like Isis, Serapis was personified with a completely human form, which helped his adoption in the Hellenistic world and Rome. It is uncertain whether Ptolemy was responsible for this very Hellenistic image of the god, for although Osiris-apis did exist before he re-created him as Serapis, we have no verifiable earlier images of his shape. While Serapis did gain acceptance in Rome (the emperor Vespasian even put his likeness on a coin), he was usually worshiped in conjunction with Isis – a goddess whom Serapis never matched in stature, despite the intentions of his creators.

This was not for lack of trying. One of Ptolemy's successors – Ptolemy III – built Serapis a magnificent temple in Alexandria which became a centre of cult worship. So much so, in fact, that many people saw the violent destruction of the Alexandrian Serapaeum in the late fourth century as symbolic of the overall triumph of Christianity.

ASCLEPIUS
⚔
AESCULAPIUS

Lord Asclepius, kindest of all gods to mankind, wormwood cannot
be compared to your powers (and never would I attempt to claim
such a thing). But in wormwood we are reminded of your
munificence and your amazing power to heal.

Aelian on the herb Artemesia, *De Animalia* 9.33

As medicine became more of a science the Greeks and Romans
became aware that actual treatment of a malady was more
effective than prayer alone. Nevertheless, they felt that religion
and healing were very much intertwined and for this reason they
turned their attention upon a character called Aesculapius (or
Asclepius). The Greeks and Romans had differing opinions as
to how this man became a god. For the Greeks, Asclepius was
born human – well, semi-human – and achieved divinity through
his exceptional efforts. This was a path trodden by others such
as Heracles and Dionysus, who were originally considered more
mortal than divine.

For the Romans matters were more straightforward.
Aesculapius was the perfect doctor and perfection was divine by
definition. Since he represented the paradigm towards which all
lesser doctors should strive, that settled the question in Roman
minds – Aesculapius was a god.

Rather like Dionysus, Asclepius had an extremely fraught
birth. His mother, Coronis, was one of the doomed loves of
Apollo (see pp. 141–42). Coronis was already pregnant when
she decided that she preferred having a human lover to the
perilous position of paramour to a Greek god. Apollo did not

Robinet Testard, Asclepius, from Évrart de Conty's *Les Échecs amoureux moralisés*, 15th century.

—

This depiction of Asclepius shows him in contemporary dress as a somewhat monkish doctor, but carrying his identifying staff with entwined snake as he examines a potion.

take rejection well and he promptly had Coronis killed. It was only when the body was placed upon its funeral pyre that Apollo noticed there was a child within, and with seconds to spare he performed a record-breaking caesarean upon the corpse.

It is from these pre-natal adventures that the Greeks reckoned Asclepius got his name – which they considered to mean 'cut out' (the 'a' prefix meaning 'out' and the 'sclepius' from the same root that gives 'scalpel' and 'sculptor'). Since the Greeks and Romans were great believers in nature over nurture, they thought that Asclepius had an inborn talent for medicine. His father was, after all, Apollo, the god who inflicts plagues but also stops them.

Perhaps Apollo felt the same way, for he placed the young Asclepius in the care of the foremost medical practitioner of the day – the centaur Chiron. While the average centaur was a wild, semi-feral creature with a low tolerance for alcohol, Chiron was an altogether different breed. (Literally – most centaurs had a human torso on a horse's body. Chiron was more of a human who had a horse's hindquarters where most people have buttocks.)

Although Chiron's medical skills were renowned, unfortunately they were no match for the deadly poison of the

Hydra, and he perished after being accidentally skewered by a poison-tipped arrow fired by Heracles. The lamentable fate of his great tutor may have inspired Asclepius to greater feats of medical skill, for thereafter there was no stopping him. No matter what their condition, any patient brought to Asclepius was speedily restored to health – to the extent that Hades became alarmed at the rapidly diminishing number of arrivals in the underworld.

Asclepius might have escaped unpunished had he not pushed the boundaries of medicine beyond acceptable limits. The legend says that snakes would come to him and whisper forbidden knowledge into his ear (in the ancient world snakes were keepers of wisdom and arcane secrets). On one such occasion a snake started to ascend to Asclepius' shoulder by climbing the staff that he had beside him. Asclepius was distracted at the time and startled when he glimpsed slithery movement out of the corner of his eye. Acting on reflex, he slew the snake. He then stood distraught over the corpse until another snake slithered up with a herb in its mouth, which it placed against the nostrils

Attributed to Johann König, after Adam Elsheimer, *Apollo and Coronis*, c. 1607.
–
In this painting a desperate Apollo tries to revive Coronis, who lies dead but pregnant with the still living foetus of Asclepius. That Apollo's efforts are in vain is shown by the dead branches of the tree above and the funeral pyre in the background.

of its deceased companion. The herb miraculously restored life to the victim. Asclepius had found the means to cheat death itself.

However, in the world of myth Death (Thanatos) was a real being who did not appreciate being cheated. Once Asclepius started to raise the dead, Thanatos took his complaint to the highest authority. Zeus, already mindful of the complaints of Hades, decided it was time to smite the over-achieving medic with a thunderbolt. Apollo was grieved by the death of his talented son and took it out on the unfortunate Cyclops who had crafted the lethal thunderbolt (for which Apollo was punished by Zeus). Thereafter Apollo – who had already placed Asclepius among the stars with his own constellation (Ophiuchus or 'serpent-bearer') – implored Zeus to make Asclepius into a god.

Temples to Asclepius were as close to hospitals as most people came in the ancient world. Priests would keep petitioners to the god within the temple until they divined the correct treatment for their malady through dreams. Those who were healed departed, often leaving behind a substantial donation and a plaque recording the nature of their illness and the treatment that had relieved it.

A sceptic might note that temples of Asclepius were generally situated out of town, away from urban miasmas and open

Attributed to the Painter of London B620, oinochoe with Chiron (detail), Greek, 520–500 BC.

—

While most centaurs were savage creatures easily overwhelmed by their passions, the wise teacher Chiron was literally a different species. Rather than having a human torso growing from a horse's neck, Chiron was a (fully clothed) human with a horse's hindquarters, as shown in this late 6th-century depiction.

sewers. Fresh air, clean water and a balanced diet doubtless helped, and skilled priests probably took patients the rest of the way to recovery, especially as a true believer's body can do great things if the mind is convinced it can. At the very least patients had plenty of time to come to terms with ophidiophobia (fear of snakes) as these were commonly kept on the temple grounds and were particularly abundant in the god's principal sanctuary of Epidaurus.

Asclepius came to the attention of the Romans in 293 BC, at a time when their city was grappling with a particularly virulent plague. The senate decided to send to Epidaurus to ask for a statue of the healer god to be brought to Rome. Once the statue was aboard the ship transporting it to its new home, the crew were delighted to see that one of the sacred snakes had somehow also come along. Delight changed to panic when the snake went missing as the ship prepared to dock in Rome, but it was discovered that the creature had left the ship and swum across to the Tiber Island in the middle of the river. Since this was evidently where Asclepius wanted his

Jean-François Léonor
Mérimée, *Diana returns
Hippolytus, resurrected
by Aesculapius, to Aricia*,
1800–25.

–

According to some forms of
the myth, after being killed
by his horses, the tragic
Hippolytus was among those
whom Aesculapius restored
to life. Diana, who requested
this, stands on the right with
identifying bow and white fawn.

temple to be, the Romans built it there and the plague
promptly stopped.

The Romans seemed to believe that fiddling with a god's
name made him more one of their own, so the Greek Asclepius
became the Roman Aesculapius, though both the iconography
and origin myth of the god remained the same. The staff of
Asclepius/Aesculapius with its entwining snake symbolized
healing and the medical profession to the Greeks and Romans,
and continues to do so in most of the world today. The main
exception is the USA, where the double-snaked caduceus of
Hermes/Mercury is preferred (see p. 160).

Two of the children of the god of healing deserve further
mention. After millennia of neglect, doctors have finally come
to appreciate the importance of Asclepius' daughter Hygeia,
though the search is still on to locate Hygeia's yet more
important sister, Panacea.

MITHRAS

The apostles, as they were divinely ordered to do, wrote texts which
are called Gospels. [They tell] that Jesus broke bread, and gave thanks saying,
'Do this in memory of me'... And these things wicked devils have mirrored
in the mysteries of Mithras, ordaining that the same should be done there.

Justin, *Apologia* 1.66

Most of the gods of Greece and Rome were public figures –
indeed they have been described as 'super-citizens' of the
cities that they patronized, larger-than-life characters with
terrifying powers, but always a known quantity. Yet as we move
towards the later eras of the Roman Empire, there was a shift
to 'mystery' religions, in which the worship of the god was not
carried out in large-scale public rituals but rather in private,
almost secretive, meetings of initiates.

In fact, when we look at the original meaning of 'pagan' in
Latin, the word means the opposite of 'initiate'. A group with
specialized knowledge would refer to outsiders as 'pagans'; for
example, the Roman army used the term to describe civilians. So
while the early Christians – who followed something of a mystery
religion themselves – referred to non-Christians as 'pagans', the
followers of the god Mithras probably did the same.

What is not known about Mithras and his worshipers outweighs
by a considerable margin the few scraps of information that we
do have. We know, for example, that Mithras probably takes his
name from the very ancient god Mithra, who was worshiped in
the east even before the Persian Empire came into being. While
it is generally believed that Mithraism as a religion developed

Statue of Mithras slaying the bull, Roman, 2nd century AD.
—
This is one of numerous statues and paintings of Mithras, all of which are very much the same. Mithras wears eastern dress and a Phrygian cap and holds the bull by the nostrils. A god, snake and scorpion all play parts in the event.

in Rome in the late first century BC, the name Mithridates ('the gift of Mithra') was already common in Asia Minor for centuries before that.

We don't know how closely the worship of the reinvented Roman god Mithras resembled the worship of the ancient eastern god Mithra, because we know very little about the rites or underlying beliefs of either religion. Most information about Mithras comes from the excavation of Mithraeums where followers of the god gathered to feast in his honour. Feasting certainly happened here, because signs of large-scale cookery are abundant, yet we can only assume that religious worship happened at the same time, despite a depressing lack of evidence.

However, archaeology has established that Mithraism was a largely urban cult because Mithraeums have been discovered in most cities of the Roman Empire but almost none in villages. The prevalence of Mithraeums near army camps shows worship of the god was widespread in the Roman army, where communal worship replaced the social bonds that the soldiers had lost when they were posted away from home to distant garrisons.

The important thing about Mithras is that he killed a bull. Why he killed the bull, and what the bull symbolizes, remain a mystery although numerous theories have been put forward, usually related to themes of death and rebirth. Almost every Mithraeum has at least two things in common: the place is underground, sometimes in an actual cave, and it contains a representation of the tauroctony ('bull-slaying'). Hundreds of depictions of the tauroctony have been found and they are all remarkably similar.

Mithras (at least we assume the person doing the killing is Mithras – he could have been the bull for all we know) wears eastern dress and lifts the head of a kneeling bull by the nostrils as he stabs it in the neck. A dog and a snake are present for the killing, and for some inexplicable reason a scorpion is attacking the bull's testicles. The bull's tail ends with what appear to be sheaves of corn and Mithras looks back and up, often to an image of Sol Invictus (the unconquered sun, who was also worshiped in the later empire). In a separate scene Mithras and Sol are depicted together feasting, presumably on the remains of the bull. Another very common depiction of Mithras shows him being born from a rock – or possibly sinking back into one.

What this all means is unknown – not only are the secrets of Mithras impenetrable today, they were also concealed from contemporary non-Mithraists. Indeed, the mysteries of the religion were also held back from initiates, who had to progress up through various levels to discover more of what it was actually all about. There were apparently seven levels, from 'Crow' at the bottom to 'Father' at the top, and those seeking the ultimate truth had to endure various painful ordeals before being initiated into the next level.

There was a considerable amount of astrological or astronomical phenomena in Mithraism, and each level was linked with a planet (or with the moon and the sun, which were probably roped in to bring the levels to the sacred number of seven). One intriguing aspect of this is that the levels – excluding the sun and moon – follow the sequence of the planets' distance from the sun, with Mercury as the lowest level, then Venus, Mars, Jupiter and finally Saturn in the top tier. This is presumably coincidence, since the alternative is believing that Mithraists had worked out not only that we live in a heliocentric solar system while everyone else thought that the sun orbited the earth, but also the relative distance of each planet from the sun.

It is probably not a coincidence that the top tier of Mithraism was dedicated to Saturn, the god of death and renewal, as these were generally believed to have been themes of Mithraic worship. Early Christians were highly indignant that many of the ideas and rituals of Mithraism – including death and

Fresco with Mithras slaying
the bull, Roman, from the
Mithraeum in Marino,
2nd century AD.

—

This fresco was discovered in
1963 in a village just south of
Rome. The Mithraeum probably
dates from the 2nd century AD
and this painting was central,
overlooking benches upon
which worshipers probably
dined.

rebirth – echoed those of Christianity as a 'diabolical mockery'.
Much of what we know of Mithraic ritual comes from Christian
complaints, for example, that Mithraists used a cross within a
circle as one of their symbols, that something akin to baptism
was a Mithraic rite, and that Sol Invictus was allegedly born on
25 December. There is considerable debate about which religion
stole what from which, or whether themes in both religions
developed spontaneously from ideas of the divine prevailing in
the first century AD.

Given the similarities in belief, it is unsurprising that
Christians stamped down hard on Mithraism when they got the
chance, sometimes building churches on top of Mithraeums as a
literal sign of the supremacy of their religion. The last pagans in
Rome reacted against this, with the final non-Christians being
Roman aristocrats who turned to Mithraism as an alternative to
the monotheistic demands of the Church.

While the determined efforts of preachers never managed
fully to stamp out the worship of Isis and Hecate, Christianity had
more success with Mithraism, which had died out as a religion by
the sixth century AD. While knowledge of Mithras has vanished,
Mithraeums are still being unearthed at a remarkable rate, and
Londoners, for example, need only to go to 12 Walbrook St, EC4,
to visit a Mithraeum restored to something like the condition in
which the last worshipers left it.

Fresco with Apollo holding
a cithara (lyre), Roman,
1st century AD.

–

The Greek styling of the
figure and the support of a
statuette nearby suggest that
this painting is based upon an
earlier sculpture.

Between Human and Divine

In the world of myth there was no hard and fast line between
men and their gods – gods and humans interbred regularly and
the result of their union might go on to become a (relatively)
normal mortal, a hero, or even join the gods on Olympus. It
helped of course that an upstanding moral character was not a
qualification – the only criterion was that if one achieved feats
beyond those of a normal mortal, one was probably divine.

This thinking extended from the early myths into the classical
era where, for example, the Athenians decided that the very
human Demetrius Poliorcetes was divine on account of his
military achievements. This was despite the fact that Demetrius
was inordinately fond of wine and women, and drank himself
to death (or back to heaven) while in his forties. The Romans
also happily immortalized their leading citizens. Their fratricidal
founder Romulus became the god Quirinus upon his death,
while Julius Caesar and Augustus set the precedent that led to
dead emperors automatically taking a place in the heavens.

Numa, the legendary second king of Rome, allegedly had
a platonic friendship with a nymph called Egeria who taught
him how best to approach the gods through religion and sacred
rites. Egeria could do this because nymphs always interacted
freely – sometimes very freely – with both men and gods,
and were therefore something of a conduit between the two.
Consider, for example, Thetis, whom Zeus considered seducing
until he discovered that she was destined to bear a son greater
than his father. This led to Thetis being rapidly demoted from a
possible paramour of the greatest of the gods to the hastily wed
wife of a normal mortal. (Her son, Achilles, did indeed outshine
his father during his brief but violent life.)

Thetis was a Nereid, which could be roughly described as a
nymph of the sea, and though she was senior among her kind
she was not exceptional in moving between what today we
would call the natural and supernatural worlds. She could do so
because this distinction barely existed in antiquity.

Few of us today have seen a narwhal, yet we readily believe
that they do exist. Yet a whale with a unicorn's horn on its
forehead is intrinsically less credible than, for example, a

dryad. The Greeks and Romans saw no reason not to believe in both – and more besides. Dryads were the spiritual essence of a tree – often an oak or laurel – and it is a rare human who has walked through a forest in the wilderness and not felt the presence of something more than human. Such feelings came even more easily to the Greeks and Romans. For them the world was numinous. That is, there was no distinction between natural and divine because the divine *was* natural. Everything in nature had its own spirit, be it a grove or a pool, and these spirits had greater gods who looked after them (the Greeks and especially the Romans were very hierarchical).

When a farmer saw the seeds that he had put into the ground turn into a flourishing field of wheat, thanking the force that had created this natural bounty was not so much an act of worship as basic good manners. And while giving thanks, the farmer might consider dropping a few hints to the sky gods that a bit of rain soon might be welcome.

In short, the gods of Greece and Rome were not remote, distant and separate from humanity. They were an integral part of daily life, fellow inhabitants of the cosmos. They were part of a spectrum of living beings that started from somewhere below the ants and stretched uninterrupted right up to Zeus atop Mount Olympus, and all these parts of the spectrum interacted with one another. Humans were somewhere around the middle of the scale and not particularly special. Thanks to their poor impulse control, centaurs and satyrs ranked slightly below humanity, nymphs somewhat above, but all, even the great gods, shared what we – with our poverty of inclusive language – can only describe as a common humanity.

Today we tend to place human, natural and divine in separate mental compartments, and kinship with the whole is considered something that can only be achieved through special circumstances or specific acts of meditation. It is no longer true that such a state of mind is simply taken for granted. The assumption that one is a natural part of a greater whole, fully integrated into the universe, is perhaps the greatest gift that the gods of Greece and Rome gave to their followers.

FURTHER READING

Original Greek and Roman texts
Anonymous, *The Orphic Hymns*
Cicero, *De Natura Deorum*
Hesiod, *Theogony*
Homer, *Iliad* and *Odyssey*
Hyginus, *Fabulae*
Lucretius, *De Rerum Natura*
Ovid, *Metamorphoses*
Pliny the Elder, *Historia Naturalis*
Pseudo-Apollodorus, *Bibliotheca*
Virgil, *Aeneid*

Commentary
Alcock, S. & Osborne, R., (eds) *Placing the Gods, Sanctuaries and Sacred Space in Ancient Greece*, Clarendon Press, Oxford, 1994

Allan, W., 'Religious Syncretism: The New Gods of Greek Tragedy', *Harvard Studies in Classical Philology*, vol. 102, pp. 113–55, 2004

Clark, A., 'Roman Gods. A Conceptual Approach', *The Classical Review*, vol. 60, no. 2, pp. 515–17, 2010

Edmunds, L. (ed.), *Approaches to Greek Myth*, Johns Hopkins University Press, Baltimore, 1990

Eidinow, E. & Kindt, J., *Oxford Handbook of Ancient Greek Religion*, Oxford University Press, Oxford, 2016

Fantham, E. & Fairey, E., *Roman Religion*, Oxford Bibliographies Online, Oxford, 2010

Graves, R., *The Greek Myths*, Penguin, London, 1996

Matyszak, P., *The Greek and Roman Myths*, Thames & Hudson, 2010

Pedley, J., *Sanctuaries and the Sacred in the Ancient Greek World*, University of Michigan, Ann Arbor, 2005

Rüpke, J. (ed.), *A Companion to Roman Religion*, Wiley, New York, 2011

Sources of quotations/references in the text
All translations of ancient literary quotations are the author's own.

p. 35 Ovid, *Metamorphoses* 10: 155; Horace, *Odes* 4.4; and Virgil, *Aen.* 5.252

p. 51 Homer, *Iliad* 1: 404ff

p. 59 Ovid, *Fasti* 4: 865–71

p. 102 Arnobius of Sicca, *Adversos Gentes* 2

p. 129 Homer, *Odyssey* 11: 580

p. 153 Virgil, *Aeneid* 8: 134 ff

p. 158 Aesop, *Fables* 519

p. 160 Pseudo-Hyginus, *Astronomica* 2.7

p. 166 Apollodorus, frag. p. 1056

p. 205 Martial, *Epigrams* 8.2

p. 241 Ambrosiaster, *Quaestiones veteris et novi testamenti* 113: 11

SOURCES OF ILLUSTRATIONS

a = above, b = below, c = centre, l= left, r = right

2 The J. Paul Getty Museum, Los Angeles; 4l Musée du Louvre, Paris. Photo RMN-Grand Palais (musée du Louvre)/Hervé Lewandowski; 4r Palazzo Gessi, Faenza. Photo Mondadori Portfolio/Getty Images; 5l Palazzo del Te, Mantua. Photo akg-images/Erich Lessing; 5r Staatliche Antikensammlungen, Munich. Photo Scala, Florence/bpk, Bildagentur für Kunst, Kultur und Geschichte, Berlin; 6–7 Map drawn by Drazen Tomic; 8–9 Archaeological Museum of Ancient Corinth. Photo Superstock/Peter Eastland/age fotostock; 10 Palazzo del Te, Mantua. Photo akg-images/Erich Lessing; 12 Sammlung Archiv für Kunst und Geschichte, Berlin. Photo akg-images; 13 Private collection; 15 The Metropolitan Museum of Art, New York. Purchase by subscription, 1896; 16 Neues Museum, Berlin (work now destroyed). Photo Bildarchiv Foto Marburg/Uwe Gaasch; 18–19 Palazzo del Te, Mantua. Photo akg-images/Erich Lessing; 20 Yale University Art Gallery, New Haven. Leonard C. Hanna, Jr, Class of 1913, Fund; 23 The Cleveland Museum of Art. Gift of the John Huntington Art and Polytechnic Trust 1915.559; 27 Museu Nacional Arqueològic de Tarragona. Photo Prisma Archivo/Alamy Stock Photo; 28 SMK – Statens Museum for Kunst, Copenhagen; 31 The British Museum, London. Photo The Trustees of the British Museum; 33 Private collection; 34 Photo De Agostini/A. Dagli Orti via Getty Images; 35 Musée du Louvre, Paris. Photo RMN-Grand Palais (musée du Louvre)/Hervé Lewandowski; 36–37 The Metropolitan Museum of Art, New York. Rogers Fund, 1910. Photo The Metropolitan Museum of Art/Art Resource/Scala, Florence; 38 The Metropolitan Museum of Art, New York. Rogers Fund, 1914; 39 Villa Torlonia, Rome. Photo Eric Vandeville/akg-images; 41 Photo by Carlo Hermann/Kontrolab/LightRocket via Getty Images; 42l National Archaeological Museum, Naples. Photo A. Dagli Otri /Stefano Ravera/age fotostock; 42r Villa Valmarana ai Nani, Vicenza. Photo Ghigo Roli/Bridgeman Images; 45 Musée du Louvre, Paris. Photo Musée du Louvre, Dist. RMN-Grand Palais/Hervé Lewandowski; 46l The Metropolitan Museum of Art, New York. Fletcher Fund, 1928; 46r Rhode Island School of Design Museum, Providence. Museum Appropriation Fund 25.078. Courtesy of the RISD Museum, Providence, RI; 48 Private collection; 49 Patrimonio Nacional, Madrid. Photo Science History Images/Alamy Stock Photo; 51 The National Gallery, London. Photo c/A. Burkatovski/Fine Art Images; 52 Palazzo Te, Mantua. Photo Scala, Florence; 53 Bibliothèque de Genève; 54 National Archaeological Museum, Naples; 55 Pinacoteca Malaspina, Pavia. Photo DeAgostini/Superstock; 57 The British Museum, London; 58 Photo oversnap/Getty Images; 59 The British Museum, London. Photo The Trustees of the British Museum; 60 Aphrodisias Museum, Aydın. Photo Carlos Delgado; 61 Musée du Louvre, Paris; 62–63 Palazzo Schifanoia, Ferrara; 64 Musée du Louvre, Paris. Photo Musée du Louvre, Dist. RMN-Grand Palais/Martine Beck-Coppola; 65 The Metropolitan Museum of Art, New York. Rogers Fund, 1914; 67 Musée national du Bardo, Tunis. Photo akg-images/Gilles Mermet; 68 Museo Barracco de Escultura Antigua, Rome; 69 Museum Boijmans Van Beuningen, Rotterdam. Acquired with the collection of D.G. van Beuningen 1958. Photo Studio Tromp; 71 Palazzo Vecchio Museum, Florence; 72l The Metropolitan Museum of Art, New York. Fletcher Fund, 1956; 72r The Metropolitan Museum of Art, New York. Rogers Fund, 1906; 73 British Library, London. Photo British Library Board. All Rights Reserved/Bridgeman Images; 74–75 Museo del Prado, Madrid. Photo Museo Nacional del Prado/Scala, Florence; 77 Vatican Museums, Vatican City. Photo akg-images/Erich Lessing; 78 National Archaeological Museum, Paestum. Photo Scala, Florence – courtesy of the Ministero Beni e Att. Culturali e del Turismo; 80–81 Yale Center for British Art, New Haven. Paul Mellon Collection; 82 Museo Archeologico Nazionale di Reggio Calabria. Photo akg-images/Andrea Baguzzi; 83 Galleria Estense, Modena. Photo akg-images/Ghigo Roli; 84 Museo del Prado, Madrid. Photo Museo Nacional del Prado/Scala, Florence; 87 Photo Superstock/James Hardy/PhotoAlto; 88–89 Neue Pinakothek, Bayerische Staatsgemäldesammlungen, Munich. Photo Scala, Florence/bpk, Bildagentur für Kunst, Kultur und Geschichte, Berlin; 91 Photo Superstock/DeAgostini; 92 The Metropolitan Museum of Art, New York. Rogers Fund, 1917; 93 The Metropolitan Museum of

Art, New York. Rogers Fund, 1923; **94–95** Vatican Museums, Vatican City. Photo Peter Barritt/Superstock; **96** The Metropolitan Museum of Art, New York. The Bothmer Purchase Fund, 1993; **97** The British Museum, London. Photo The Trustees of the British Museum; **98** Staatliche Kunstsammlungen, Dresden. Photo BPK, Berlin, Dist. RMN-Grand Palais/Elke Estel/Hans-Peter Klut; **101** Photo Stefano Ravera/Alamy Stock Photo; **103** Villa Farnesina, Rome. Photo Araldo De Luca; **104** British Library, London. Photo British Library Board. All Rights Reserved/Bridgeman Images; **105** Musée du Louvre, Paris. Photo RMN-Grand Palais (musée du Louvre)/Hervé Lewandowski; **107** Galleria Borghese, Rome. Photo © Andrea Jemolo/Bridgeman Images; **108** Piccolomini Library, Duomo, Siena. Photo Ghigo Roli/Bridgeman Images; **109** The Metropolitan Museum of Art, New York. Gift of Miss Matilda W. Bruce, 1907; **110** The Metropolitan Museum of Art, New York. Rogers Fund, 1914; **112** Palazzo Gessi, Faenza. Photo Mondadori Portfolio/Getty Images; **114** National Archaeological Museum, Naples. Photo Superstock/Universal Images Group; **116** Musée du Louvre, Paris. Photo RMN-Grand Palais (musée du Louvre)/Stéphane Maréchalle; **117** Vienna Museum; **118** Harris Museum and Art Gallery, Preston. Photo Harris Museum and Art Gallery/Bridgeman Images; **120** The Cleveland Museum of Art. Leonard C. Hanna, Jr Fund 1982.142; **121** The Metropolitan Museum of Art, New York. Rogers Fund, 1912; **122** British Library, London. Photo British Library Board. All Rights Reserved/Bridgeman Images; **124** Villa Farnesina, Rome. Photo Adam Eastland/Alamy Stock Photo; **125al** The Metropolitan Museum of Art, New York. Fletcher Fund, 1931; **125ar** The British Museum, London. Photo The Trustees of the British Museum; **125c** The Cleveland Museum of Art. Gift of Robert Haber 1996.34; **125b** The Metropolitan Museum of Art, New York. Harris Brisbane Dick Fund, 1939; **126** Photo G. Nimatallah/De Agostini via Getty Images; **128** Los Angeles County Museum of Art. The Phil Berg Collection (M.71.73.99); **131** Musée du Louvre, Paris. Photo Musée du Louvre, Dist. RMN-Grand Palais/Thierry Ollivier; **132** Photo Fine Art Photographic Library/Corbis via Getty Images; **134** The Fitzwilliam Museum, Cambridge. Photo

Fitzwilliam Museum/Bridgeman Images; **135** Palazzo Giustiniani Odescalchi, Bassano Romano; **137** Ephesus Archaeological Museum, Selçuk. Photo Roland and Sabrina Michaud/akg-images; **139** Smithsonian American Art Museum, Washington, D.C. Transfer from the National Institute; **140** The National Gallery, London. Photo Bridgeman Images; **143** The National Gallery, London; **144** Mauritshuis, The Hague; **145** Belvedere, Vienna; **147** Museo Palatino, Rome. Photo Werner Forman/Universal Images Group/Getty Images; **148–49** Museum of Fine Arts, Boston. Bartlett Collection—Museum purchase with funds from the Francis Bartlett Donation of 1912 and Picture Fund. Photo Museum of Fine Arts, Boston. All rights reserved/Scala, Florence; **151** The British Museum, London. Photo The Trustees of the British Museum; **152** The Uffizi, Florence. Photo akg-images/Rabatti & Domingie; **153** The Metropolitan Museum of Art, New York. Fletcher Fund, 1925; **154** Rijksmuseum, Amsterdam; **155** National Academy of San Luca, Rome. Photo Fine Art Images/Heritage Images/Getty Images; **156–57** The Walters Art Museum, Baltimore; **159** Palazzo Clerici, Milan. Photo Scala, Florence/Mauro Ranzani; **160l** National Gallery of Art, Washington, D.C. Rosenwald Collection; **160r** Kunstmuseum Basel; **161** Photo akg-images/Science Source; **163** Musée du Louvre, Paris. Photo Musée du Louvre, Dist. RMN-Grand Palais/Thierry Ollivier; **164** Collegio del Cambio, Perugia. Photo Scala, Florence; **165** Kunstmuseum Basel; **166–67** Musée du Louvre, Paris. Photo RMN-Grand Palais (musée du Louvre)/Hervé Lewandowski; **168l** The J. Paul Getty Museum, Los Angeles. Gift of Barbara and Lawrence Fleischman; **168r** The J. Paul Getty Museum, Los Angeles; **169l** Vatican Museums, Vatican City. Photo G. Nimatallah/De Agostini via Getty Images; **169r** Musée du Louvre, Paris. Photo Musée du Louvre, Dist. RMN-Grand Palais/Hervé Lewandowski; **170** National Archaeological Museum, Naples; **172–73** The National Gallery, London; **175** National Museum of Bargello, Florence. Photo © Arte & Immagini srl/Corbis via Getty Images; **176** Archaeological Museum of Delos. Photo Art Images via Getty Images; **179a** Harvard Art Museums/Arthur M. Sackler Museum, Cambridge, MA. Gift of Dr Harris Kennedy, Class of 1894. Photo

© President and Fellows of Harvard College, 1932.56.39; **179bl** The Metropolitan Museum of Art, New York. Fletcher Fund, 1956; **179br** The Metropolitan Museum of Art, New York. Purchase by subscription, 1896; **180** The Cleveland Museum of Art. Bequest of Noah L. Butkin 1980.238; **181** Worcester Art Museum; **182–83** Photo © Adriano Spano/ Dreamstime.com; **184** Staatliche Antikensammlungen, Munich. Photo Scala, Florence/bpk, Bildagentur für Kunst, Kultur und Geschichte, Berlin; **185l** The British Museum, London. Photo The Trustees of the British Museum; **185r** The Cleveland Museum of Art. John L. Severance Fund 1989.73; **186** The Metropolitan Museum of Art, New York. Rogers Fund, 1912; **187** National Archaeological Museum, Naples. Photo Carole Raddato; **189** Galleria Nazionale d'Arte Moderna, Rome. Photo Alessandro Vasari/ Archivio Vasari/Mondadori Portfolio via Getty Images; **191** Royal Palace of La Granja of San Ildefonso. Photo akg-images/Science Source; **192** Private collection; **193** Antikensammlung, Staatliche Museen zu Berlin; **194** Kunsthistorisches Museum, Vienna. Photo akg-images/Erich Lessing; **197** Museum of Art and Archaeology, University of Missouri; **198** Photo Peter Horree/Alamy Stock Photo; **201** National Archaeological Museum, Naples. Photo Scala, Florence; **203** Museo Nazionale Etrusco di Villa Giulia, Rome. Photo Scala, Florence; **204** The J. Paul Getty Museum, Los Angeles; **206** Musée Condé, Chantilly. Photo by PHAS/Universal Images Group via Getty Images; **207** Art Institute of Chicago. Gift of William F. Dunham; **209** The Metropolitan Museum of Art, New York. The Bothmer Purchase Fund, 1987; **211** Museum of Fine Arts, Boston. Bartlett Collection—Museum purchase with funds from the Francis Bartlett Donation of 1900. Photo Museum of Fine Arts, Boston. All rights reserved/ Scala, Florence; **212l** Musée du Louvre, Paris. Photo Musée du Louvre, Dist. RMN-Grand Palais/Georges Poncet; **212r** The J. Paul Getty Museum, Los Angeles; **213** The British Museum, London. Photo The Trustees of the British Museum; **214** Musée du Louvre, Paris. Photo Musée du Louvre, Dist. RMN-Grand Palais/ Thierry Ollivier; **215** Tate. Presented by W. Graham Robertson 1939; **217** Photo © Fondazione Torlonia. Photo Lorenzo De Masi; **218** Dumbarton Oaks Museum, Washington, D.C.; **219** SMK – Statens Museum for Kunst, Copenhagen; **220** Palazzo Maffei, Verona. Photo Sergio Anelli/Electa/ Mondadori Portfolio via Getty Images; **221** Musée des Beaux-Arts, Chambéry. Photo RMN-Grand Palais/Thierry Ollivier; **222** National Archaeological Museum, Naples; **225** Private collection; **226** National Archaeological Museum, Naples; **227** National Archaeological Museum, Naples. Photo akg-images; **229** The British Museum. Photo The Trustees of the British Museum; **230** The British Museum. Photo The Trustees of the British Museum; **233** Bibliothèque nationale de France, Paris. Photo BnF, Dist. RMN-Grand Palais/image BnF; **234** Agnes Etherington Art Centre, Kingston, Ontario. Gift of Alfred and Isabel Bader, 2014; **235** The British Museum, London. Photo The Trustees of the British Museum; **236–37** Musée du Louvre, Paris. Photo RMN-Grand Palais (musée du Louvre)/Adrien Didierjean; **239** The British Museum, London. Photo The Trustees of the British Museum; **241** Photo Granger Historical Picture Archive/Alamy Stock Photo; **242** The British Museum, London. Photo The Trustees of the British Museum

Page references in *italics* refer to illustrations.

Aachen 97
Aborigines 205
Abrahamic faiths 11, 14
Achilles *72*, *96*, *118*, 192, *193*, 196, 243
Acropolis 117, 124; Athenian 124, 196
Actaeon *132*, 133
Admetus 142
Adonis 67, 68, 133
Aegean Sea 91, 130, 178, 190, 223
Aelian Animalia 86, 232
Aeneas 54, 60, *60*, *61*, *80*, 158, 196, 218
Aeschylus 184
Aesculapius/Asclepius 141, 201, 232–37, *233*, *234–46*
Aesop (writer) 158
Afghanistan 223
Africa 35, 158
Agamemnon, king 118, 134, *135*
Alba Longa 219
Alcmene 53
Alexander the Great 200, 223, 228, 231
Alexandria 224, 228, 231
Amalthea 33
America 35, 160, 237
Amnisos 127
Amphitrite 91, *91*; *see also* Poseidon
Amphitryon 53
Anath 58; *see also* Aphrodite
Anatolia 152, 174
Anchises *60*

Anteros 66, 171
Anubis *226*
Apennines 86
Aphrodite/Venus 15, 21, 25, 27, 40, 53, 56, 58–61, *57–65*, *64*–68, *67*, 100, *116*, 123, 133, *134*, 148, 154, 155, 158, 170, *170*, *172*, *173*, *192*, 193, 194, *194*, *225*, 226, 240; *aphros* 61; Genetrix 61; Obsequens 56; Pandemos 67; Porne 68; Nana 100; Tosanoides 65; Verticordia 68; Vulgivaga 67
Aphrodisias/Stauropolis *60*
Apis Bull 231; *see also* Osiris
Aplu 141; *see also* Apollo
Apollo 14, 21, *23*, 40, 66, 68, 129, 130, 132, 133, 138, 140–42, *140*, 144–46, *143–45*, *147*, 148, 149, *149*, 153–55, 215, 232, 233, *234*, *235*, *242*; Apollonian Games 145; Apollyon 138; Atepomarus 148; Belvedere *139*; Cunomaglus 148; Delphinus 144; Medicus 145; Phoebus 146
Apollodorus 166
Apollonius Rhodius Argonautica 127
Apuleius, *The Golden Ass* 223
Aqua Virgo *87*
Aquarius (constellation) 92
Arachne *122*, 123; *see also* Athena
Archilochus (poet) 123

Areopagus 166
Ares/Mars 15, 40, 52, *64*, 65, 66, 68, 79, 100, 122, 119, 162, 164–67, *164*, *165*, *168–70*, 170, 171–73, *172*, *173*, 188, 194, 240; Mars Ultor 164; Borgese *163*
Argos 53
Argus Panoptes 14, 48, *48*, 154–57, *155*, *156*
Ariadne 178, 180, *181*
Arion 96
Aristophanes playwright 184
Arnobius Adversos Gentes 102
Artemis/Diana 14, 40, 68, 100, *126*, 127, *128*, 129, 130, *131*, 132, *132*, 133–36, *134*, *135*, *137*, 138, 142, 148, 210, 211, 213, 214, 226, *235*, *236*; Temple at Ephesus 136; Artemesia 232
Arval Brotherhood 167
Asclepius *see* Aesculapius
Asia 39, 129, 135, 136, 141, 148, 152, 208, 210, 239
asphodel 77
Assisi, Italy 124
Assyrians *64*, 100
Astarte/Ishtar 58, 65, 68
Athena/Minerva 14, 21, *23*, 32, *36*, 43, 47, 48, 50, 53, *64*, 65, 66, *72*, 92, 93, 98, *98*, 99, 102, 115–17, *116*, 118, 119, 120, *120–22*, 122–24, 127, 129, 138, 158, 162, 165, 167, 171, 188, 190, 193, *197*, 210, 226; aegis of *114*, 120, 125; Ergane 122,

Frontispiece: Mosaic Floor with Head of Medusa, Roman, *c.* 115–150.
The J. Paul Getty Museum, Los Angeles
Page 28: After Guido Reni, *The Fall of the Giants*, 1590–1642.
SMK – Statens Museum for Kunst, Copenhagen
Page 112: Felice Giani, Vault of the Hall of Diana, Palace Gessi, Faenza, 1813.
Photo Mondadori Portfolio/Getty Images
Page 198: Hecate fresco, from the Villa of Publius Fannius Synistor,
Boscoreale, Roman, *c.* 50–40 BC. Peter Horree/Alamy Stock Photo
Endpapers: Walter Crane, *Neptune's Horses*, 1892. Neue Pinakothek,
Bayerische Staatsgemäldesammlungen, Munich. Photo Scala, Florence/bpk,
Bildagentur für Kunst, Kultur und Geschichte, Berlin

First published in the United Kingdom in 2022 by
Thames & Hudson Ltd, 181A High Holborn, London WC1V 7QX

First published in the United States of America in 2022 by
Thames & Hudson Inc., 500 Fifth Avenue, New York, New York 10110

The Gods and Goddesses of Greece and Rome
© 2022 Thames & Hudson Ltd, London

Text © 2022 Philip Matyszak

Design by April

All Rights Reserved. No part of this publication may be reproduced
or transmitted in any form or by any means, electronic or mechanical,
including photocopy, recording or any other information storage and
retrieval system, without prior permission in writing from the publisher.

British Library Cataloguing-in-Publication Data
A catalogue record for this book is available from the British Library

Library of Congress Control Number 2022931879

ISBN 978-0-500-02418-8

Printed in China by RR Donnelley

Be the first to know about our new releases,
exclusive content and author events by visiting
thamesandhudson.com
thamesandhudsonusa.com
thamesandhudson.com.au